Strategy Daddy

By Michael Keesee & Ankesh Kothari

Praise for Strategy Daddy

"In this book Michael and Ankesh explain practical theories of marketing, then provide more than 100 real-world examples of those theories in action. If you use only one of these ideas, you'll find Strategy Daddy to be your best marketing investment of the year."

— Chuck McKay, Speaker, Researcher, Consultant,
Author of Fishing for Customers and Reeling Them In,
and What Ever Happened to Bennigans

"In my years in the advertising business, I have seen and heard tons of marketing horror stories. I wish this book existed back then. We'd all have saved ourselves a lot of grief."

— Tom Parsons, General Manager
Time Warner Cable Media Sales

"Michael has a talent for noting the marketing differences that make one product successful while a similar product bombs. Plus, he's a great storyteller. And that's what sets this book apart. It's immediately engaging, thought-provoking and will have your own ideas bubbling to the surface within a few pages. I've had a hard time putting it down—but I've had to, in order to make notes on ideas it's given me for use with my own clients. I highly recommend it to anyone who needs creative marketing inspiration."

— Susan L. Cook, Principal, COOK | A Creative Consultancy
Past President, American Advertising Federation – Fort Worth
Past Governor, American Advertising Federation – Tenth District

"In Strategy Daddy, Michael Keesee has assembled a series of marketing strategies that are broadly applicable and deeply relevant. Any business owner or marketing manager would benefit from reading – and applying – the strategies that Michael has expertly introduced in this book."

— Mat Harris, CEO
BizGreet, Inc. – personalize every video

"Whether you're a senior level, entry level or any level of business or marketing professional … here's an enjoyable, must-read book for all those that understand that strategy is the 'most important thing' in marketing. Keesee and Kothari have taken a huge step to becoming to small business strategy what Trout and Reiss have been to national business strategy."

— Keith I. Mandish, Former VP Strategic Planning,
JWT & McCann-Erickson

"You won't find inane head speak in this book. This is real world fix the client problem marketing. Plus the bite size chapters make this work a useful reference long after the first read. The artful madness that is marketing is alive and well in this book."

— JP Engelbrecht, CEO
South Central Communications

"I've always looked forward to seeing Michael again and hearing another of his stories. I'm so glad he has put them in book form so we can all enjoy his wonderful perspective on this crazy world we call advertising."

— Blake Goldston
Governor, American Advertising Federation – District 10
Member, Board of Directors, American Advertising Federation
Owner, Money Mailer of Greater Amarillo

Acknowledgments

From Michael

My first thanks goes to my God. As He continues to author the story of my life, I am amazed daily and very humbled at the wonderful blessings He keeps writing in for the protagonist (me). I certainly don't deserve them.

I want to thank my family. I have been blessed to have a mom, dad and sister whose support and love has been critical to pursuing my dreams. The support from the rest of my family has been grand as well.

I also had friends like Ryan, Scott, Reny, Tiny, Blake, Jacobo, Ski, Jared, Mary, Candace, Susan, Amy, MG, BJ and Alicia…and the rest of the VLA crew who kept me sane during the process (and by sane, I mean "supplied with beer and wine").

Two people who were instrumental in this project even seeing the light of day are Justin McCullough and Ankesh Kothari. Ankesh's keen understanding of strategy gave me a friend and a mentor as we moved through this process together. Justin's motivation, determination, friendship and drill sergeanting (I don't think that's really a word) kept me on task, because Lord knows I can get lost in one of my Jimmy Buffett daydreams.

My thanks are endless for Roy Williams, the Wizard of Ads…as a mentor, partner and motivator. He invited me to join the elite Wizard Partners Marketing team. I was and am still humbled to this day to be a part of this exclusive family.

I owe the world to the most incredible group of professional friends who selflessly allowed me to siphon greatness from them as I grew as a marketer; JP Engelbrecht, Chuck McKay, Mike Dandridge, Clay Campbell, Tom Walters and Steven Sorensen, just to name a few of my closest.

In the industry, there are a few people who definitely gave me the insight to grow and guided me along the way. The Drewry Station group; Larry, Jerry,

Holly, Cindy and the rest, thank you for my start. Thanks to Ally and Michelle for pushing me forward. South Central Communications for taking a chance on an unknown. Blake Goldston, Jim Doyle and Don Fitsgibbons for encouraging me to "go for it". Susan Cook, John Aguillard and the rest of the 10th District Ad Fed Family. I am challenged constantly by the brilliance of the people that God has seen fit to put into my life. Thank you all.

I know that I am missing many people who should be on this list and I ask your forgiveness in advance. This page is undoubtedly the hardest page to write because I owe so much too so many.

"We are like dwarfs sitting on the shoulders of giants. We see more, and things that are more distant, than they did, not because our sight is superior or because we are taller than they, but because they raise us up, and by their great stature add to ours." **John of Salisbury – The Metalogicon**

Thank you to all my Giants!
Sean, Mancy and Anna…keep dreaming big!

From Anke

- Thank You for picking up this book.
- Thanks to all the marketing heroes I've learned from over the years. Especially: David Ogilvy. Rosser Reeves. Claude Hopkins. Joe Sugarman. Sean D'Souza. David Frey. Mark Joyner. Al Ries. Roy H. Williams. Jon Spoelstra. Ben Suarez. Gordon Alexander. Gary Halbert.
- Thanks to all the Marketing Hotsheet subscribers.
- Thanks to Michael Keesee for spear heading this venture and bringing it to life.
- Thanks to Mom, Dad and Sis and all my friends and extended family.

Foreword

The rather humble beginnings of this book started back in Wichita Falls when I was a Local Sales Manager for KSWO TV. When my team would meet a client we would spend a bit of time trying to find out everything we could about his or her needs. After the initial client meeting, we would sit (usually around lunch…'cause I like lunch) and discuss a client's problems, analyze the competition, the way they did business, the industry they were in and how they marketed currently.

During our discussions, we would look at the three areas that we could change to affect business. We called these three areas "In the Office, In the Store and Out the Door"…which becomes for this book the areas of business practice, the customer and the competition. I used to make notes as new techniques were created. Was there anything we could vilify, heroify, slogan tie…etc. We were making up our own techniques just so we could name things. I used to keep notes and recap some of my sales meetings (It is a rather vague translation of a sales meeting…chatting over cheese sticks and a Coke sounds so unprofessional though). Ally and Michelle suggested I start taking my notes and keeping them in a binder, as they might make a good book someday. With "good" being a relative term, there is no denying it is a book. Ankesh and I joined forces because I have always believed that you find phenomenal people and develop a friendship with them as you never know what can come out of it. Ankesh is one of those people and I am honored to call him a friend.

I hope you enjoy reading Strategy Daddy as much as I enjoyed writing it.

"A great strategy with a flawed execution will defeat a flawed strategy with an incredible execution every time." **Roy Williams – The Wizard of Ads**

Table of contents

Introduction

The typical person who grabs a marketing book will usually fall into one of three categories: A marketing salesperson who wants to get better at their craft, a marketing creative who wants to be inspired or a business owner who wants to try and find the magic bullet.

This book will help those salespeople become better at their craft, not because it will teach them sales techniques, but because it will enable them to better understand how their product helps business owners. The more they understand it, the better they will be at advising their clients toward successful marketing campaigns. Strong salespeople will see their role as a consultant and try to do anything to make their clients successful. Selling statistics and marketing one sheeters produced by some company doesn't always convince customers that marketing works. I've always found stories to be a great way to convey confidence about great marketing strategies.

The creative person will gain some methodology for producing strategy. Very often "right-brained creative" people don't always know how they come up with their ideas; they grab them from inspiration, dreams or somewhere out in left field. "Left-brained analytical" types need methodology and structure. They feel uncomfortable attempting creative or strategy without it. This book will introduce some methods for being creative in coming up with strategy. It will help the "right-brained creatives" hone their skills as much as it will help "left-brained analyticals" find some steps to unlock their creative potential.

The business people looking for the magic bullet are the trickiest. There is no magic tool that will ensure human motivation, no method that will leave its target unable to resist a message. Could you imagine the horror if this did exist? What they are really looking for is something a bit unique or outside of the box in their industry. This book will supply methods to come up with strategy for these business owners as well as lots of case studies for those methods that make it easier to adapt them to different categories. Realize that just because a case study works in one market for one specific business doesn't mean that it is universally effective. Many strategic campaigns will work for one company in a market and when the technique is used in another market, it fails miserably. Use caution when applying them.

Now I suspect that there are other people who might just dig marketing, business, advertising and strategy who pick this book up. I suspect they will get enough crazy ideas, great stories and cheeky one-liners to make the book worth their purchase.

There are two schools of thought that are en vogue about strategy. One is considered Western Strategy and the other, Eastern. Western Strategy's foundation can be found in the book "On War" by Carl Von Clausewitz. A Prussian officer during the time of Napoleon, he focused on outgunning, outnumbering and overpowering the opponent. In marketing, there are many clients who have the budgets to dominate every bit of the landscape. Their marketing strategy is to be everywhere. They tactically own every magazine, billboard, television and radio station so that there is no doubt they have name recognition and hopefully market share. The only companies that can do that strategy well are monsters like Proctor & Gamble, Coca-Cola and Microsoft. Most businesses cannot execute this strategy because the thinking that keeps these monster companies on top is not the thinking that got them there.

It would be prudent for most businesses to look more at the Eastern philosophy. Its foundation is found in "The Art of War" by Sun Tzu. The battle should be won on paper before a soldier ever steps into battle. In B. H. Liddell Hart's book "Strategy", he explains, "The true aim is not so much to seek battle as to seek a strategic situation so advantageous that if it does not of itself produce the decision, its continuation by battle is sure to achieve this." The strategy for war, like business, should be to win before it even begins.

The book is broken into three main areas:

Competition, Business, and the Customer

Competition is about strategy that relates directly to the competition. These methods and actions deal directly with how your company positions itself against the competition. Some of them are simple and some take competition to a new level. Realize that the competition for a business is not always the exact same type of store. When looking at the jewelry category, for example; before someone spends a couple thousand bucks on a ring or necklace, might they consider a big screen TV or a cruise? There is plenty of competition out there, and strategizing without being aware of the competition is a sure way to underutilize your marketing time and money.

The second area the book will focus on is the area of the business, or the business function - how the business does pricing, payments, inventory, customer services, etc. These methods will look at the actual business practices, not just the marketing. Some of the ideas are extreme, some are less wild but they are all effective ways to creatively change the battlefield. Often I'll ask, "What makes people mad about your industry?" Fix that and we have something to talk about.

The final area that we touch on in Magic Bullets is the customer category. It is about any communication that creates a touch point with the customer. This is an area that deals with how the business markets itself, taking into account the industry and customer knowledge. While these methods don't change how the business works, it may challenge the way that customers view it.

The World of Competition

Section One

So often, marketing plans and businesses are built without looking at the competitive market. How we position our business must take into account all of our competition. Now usually, we look at our immediate competitors, or those businesses that do what we do. For most businesses, there are usually a few direct rivals in the market for customer dollars. With the internet, many industries are facing worldwide competition that they have never faced before. The strategy is more important than ever. We do not do business in a vacuum nor should we strategize there.

One of my favorite stories is about a hair salon that had been on this same street for a number of years. They charged $18 for a haircut and shampoo. The owner made a good living and offered a good product. One day, a new barbershop opened up directly across the street from the old hair salon. The owner hung a sign out front that said "$6 Haircuts". The original salon owner felt the financial impact almost immediately. In the spirit of "Competitive Marketing" the original salon struck back by hanging a large sign out front that said, "We fix $6 Haircuts".

Realize that business has been compared to war many times. When it comes to fighting over customers, though, the battles are real. Many of the victories in marketing warfare go to the businesses that study their competitors and leverage the differences into advantages. I encourage clients to be well prepared and have a solid strategy planned out before entering a marketing campaign that will pit you against a competitor. Don't be unprofessional or ugly (ok, sometimes just a little); position your company against their position.

You can usually find a company's strength and use it as a weakness because the company's strength is something they will not compromise, so it is a constant. Attacking a weak point that is obvious brings the risk that they will correct the problem. A strength is something that the company does well, a characteristic of their product or service or a byproduct of their position in the market. The most important part is discovering these strengths and weaknesses in your market. Also, be aware of your own so you can decide if this is an area where you want to enter into battle.

An example of using a strength as a weakness could be a certain car rental location that advertises that there is no wait; they are free of lines. Merely by stating they don't have them, don't you start to resent having to stand in a line? Every memory of long grocery lines, countless hours of staring at the back of someone's head while you shifted weight from leg to leg comes to mind. You are so thankful that there is a company that has no wait, a company that hates lines like you do. So the next time you are offered a choice between that company and another, you will choose that company.

But here is the question: why are they free of lines? Are they free of lines because their competitor is the number one car rental location?

Are they free of lines because their cars are of lower quality or their prices are higher? They might just be free of lines because their competitor is the big dog in the market, and has lines of business. They certainly aren't going to give up that advantage so targeting the wait time makes sense for a lesser competitor. Once the strength is discovered, the campaign must then vilify lines. How is the number one location supposed to counter that?

It is important to look at your competition and find strengths and weaknesses, as well as realizing your own. A quick and easy method for finding strengths and weaknesses is the "Triangle of Destruction."

Triangle of Destruction
"Mwahahahaha Mwahaha!"

A method for finding the strengths and weaknesses in a business category is to use the "Triangle of Destruction," also called the "Good, Fast, and Cheap Trinity – You Get Two!" That is probably a more accurate name, but Triangle of Destruction sounds so much more threatening.

It is rare for a company to be successful in all three categories, as they usually sacrifice one for the other two. Are they faster, slower, busier, better service, lower cost, more expensive? Every one of these factors can be an advantage and a disadvantage. That is where the opportunity lies. Because for everything you do well, you give up something.

Good As a Weakness
(Cheap and Fast – Like I like my women?)

Not many people, when asked, would list fast food places as the highest quality food that there is. They certainly do serve their purpose and the fact that millions if not billions of dollars are spent every year on their food is a testament to their success. So does food have to be good for it to sell? It is possible that a company can succeed if it offers cheap and fast. Grocery stores have come up with "store brands" of many products that cost less than the name brand. People are willing to give up good for fast and cheap.

"We know you usually like to take the days on one at a time, but the truth is we just don't get that luxury anymore. From Soccer Moms to Homework Dads, we know that sometimes you don't have the time to plan out a meal from start to finish, cook it, eat it and clean up afterwards. When the children are screaming and you can actually feel the gray hairs growing in, give Snappy's Pizzeria a call. We'll have your meal ready lickety split. Lots-o-dough for little dough."

There are plenty of categories and competitors that use quality as an advantage. But have no fear if that isn't you or your business model - cheap and fast can certainly dominate a category. McDonald's, anyone?

Fast As a Weakness
(Good and Cheap – Like I like my women.)

Can speed be a weakness? If your competitor is the fastest, and the most inexpensive in the market, you can vilify speed by showing the importance of quality. It wouldn't take much to convince the average consumer that since you are so fast and cheap, they should consider a higher quality product or service.

"Outside of your family and your home, most people would list their car as one of their most important possessions. Here at Kleener Kars, we take the time and effort to detail your car, clean every nook and cranny and make sure it is as clean as if you took the day off to do it yourself. We know how you would treat it, so that is how we treat it, like it was our own. Would you want to take your prized possession to someone who wouldn't take the time you would on it? Bring it to us and we won't sling it through, your baby gets the royal treatment at Kleener Kars."

Kleener Kars didn't say "We do a better job, that's why we are slower" because you never want to point out a weakness as a weakness. Turn that weakness into a strength. There are many different ways to say it, but didn't the commercial just state that the car wash was Speed-Free? Speed has been turned against a competing car wash where speed was probably a selling point. This will cause people to question whether they want fast. Is quality worth the loss in time? It won't convince everyone because some people see the value in the pace. The purpose, though, was to convince a percentage, not everyone. That would be an unrealistic goal.

Cheap As a Weakness
(Fast and Good – Like I like my women!!!)

To attack a client on the fact that they are cheap, you should go after quality or speed. Obviously, use the one you are stronger in. If a client is cheaper than you are, all is not lost. I can go down the street from the Ford or Chevy dealer and just as fast, be in a BMW dealership. Not as cheap, but it scores higher in the good category. Is there a client base for a company that has higher prices, good items and no wait? Check out your local corner convenience store next time you doubt it. Because of their strength in 'fast', they can get away with losing in the cheap category.

"We've all been there. (Sound of car engine rolling over but not starting.) It can be a frightening feeling, being alone when car trouble strikes. Just know that Big Jack's Tow and Repair is there. Any time day or night, we react as if it were our own sons or daughters broken down and scared. With the fastest response time in town, you just call 555-5555 and trust that your car trouble will become our problem and not yours. When it comes to auto tows and repairs done fast and right, don't trust your family's safety to one of the creepy cheapy alternatives. Big Jack's Tow and Repair: When You Need Us, We Are There!"

In this ad, they attacked cheap by praising the virtues of fast and good. We strengthen fast and good by connecting them with safety and family. Can companies survive offering good quality products quickly, but also expensively? Quality insurance companies, safe tires for your vehicle and convenience stores make a killing doing just that!

Once the strengths and the weaknesses are discovered using the "Triangle," it's easy to start looking at the other techniques that you will use to position your company. Be sure to also look at your company and evaluate where you can be attacked. Very often this one technique, the Triangle of Destruction, will change the way you look at the world of competition. You can now start to target your efforts into a single mission, to become the home of the low prices, best items or fastest service. Realize that just saying so doesn't make it so.

Many people mistake advertising for marketing and vice versa. Marketing is the strategy. It encompasses every touch point of your business. The advertising is the bull horn that you use to shout your message to the masses.

Best of Belgium

Squashed between France and Germany lies the small country of Belgium. Belgium is known as the "King of Chocolates." For centuries, they have exported fine chocolate throughout the world. But one chocolate stands out even in Belgium: Godiva. From New York to Paris to Tokyo, it is Godiva that brings the best of Belgium to the world.

More than 75 years ago, in the year 1926, Joseph Draps opened a chocolate shop on a cobblestone street in Brussels, Belgium and named it Godiva. Draps perfected a unique formula of "rich chocolate with unparalleled smoothness." Because of the rich taste, elegant designs and beautiful packaging, Godiva became an instant hit and Draps positioned Godiva as luxury chocolate.

Since its humble beginnings in 1926, Godiva has grown a lot and has outlets around the world, with more than 1,000 outlets in America alone. Godiva conducts research every so often to gauge the taste of the diverse public. In one such study, people were asked to choose from a variety of Godiva chocolates in two different outlets.

In one outlet, a group of people was offered 6 choices and in another, a group of people was offered 30 choices. Surprisingly, those who had more choices found their selections to be less tasty, less enjoyable, and less satisfying than did those who were given limited choices.

Action Summary:

- Position your product for the higher end market and even though you may receive a lower number of sales, you will earn more.
- Limit choices to increase the perception of value.

Competing with Cheaper Copycats

Henry drops out of college in September 2002 to start his own video-editing company. To buy equipment at a low cost, he logs onto eBay.com. But soon he discovers that no one is selling the equipment he wants. So Henry finds a video equipment company that carries the products he wants. On a whim, he posts an auction for that same product the day he receives it. Eight bids and seven days later, Henry sells the video equipment for a small profit. He soon does some calculations and figures that he can make more money buying and selling hard-to-find video equipment on eBay.com than by starting his own video editing business. His calculations prove to be correct and Henry ends up selling 70 different types of video equipment for a grand total of $500,000 in gross sales within 1 year. But others get a sniff of his success and try to copy his system.

Within no time, the copycats find sources that manufacture the equipment at a much lower cost. Henry can't compete with them even when he sells the equipment at cost price making no profits. When he can't compete on a price basis, Henry decides to compete on better service. Henry starts offering free technical assistance to people who buy products from him. He starts posting his phone number in all the auction listings. Even though his prices are higher, many people choose to buy from him, as installing the complex video equipment system can be a daunting task. The sales erosion stops. But Henry doesn't stop there. He goes on and makes a step-by-step training DVD that helps buyers install and use the equipment on their own and he earns more money selling the DVDs!

Action Summary:

- Provide better service and people will be willing to pay you more.
- Give free technical assistance, and provide better customer care, and people will buy from you even though your competition is cheaper.
- Make step-by-step training tutorials on how to use your products most effectively and sell them with your products.

Technique: Armada
"You and what army?"

In 1588, the country of England was faced with a problem that many companies face today. A huge threat loomed over the horizon. A large naval fleet was heading towards England from Spain. Many companies are staring down the street as a major "category killer" is setting up shop.

There is much to be learned from how England survived and won the day. The method by which sea battles were waged in the time of the Spanish Armada was that two ships would pull parallel to each other and start firing large caliber short-range cannons at each other's ships. Then soldiers would board and fight hand to hand until the battle was over. You have no doubt seen these examples in the movies.

There were over 150 giant Spanish galleon ships bent on defeating the English. The English ships available were smaller and couldn't fight the Spaniards in the manner that battles were fought or it would have been disastrous. The rules of war would have to change, and England was going to change them. If they couldn't match the Armada with strength, they would use speed and distance.

Since the smaller English vessels couldn't match the Spanish with large guns, they had to carry fewer and smaller caliber cannons. These cannons didn't do the damage that the larger ones did, but they did fire farther. The large hulking galleon ships were formidable foes if they ever pulled up next to a ship, so England's strategy was to always stay perpendicular and far ahead, much like the shape of a T.

The strategy was to make maneuvers that the Armada was too big to counter and to shoot at ranges that the Armada would be wasting its ammunition if it tried to match. Long story short, the English defeated the Spanish Armada. The remaining Spanish fleet headed back to Spain, was hit by some terrible storms and was almost wiped out. This led to the fall of Spain as a world power. Don't expect the "category killers" or the "big guys" in your category to be destroyed, but there is no reason you have to lie down and give up just because you're a smaller business.

Size Does Matter

M. G. was starting out in his own financial planning business. He was going to be going up against some giants in the industry, some of them in the same building that his office was in. Many large companies get you as a client, put your account on a direct withdraw and then never talk to you again. Much of your future correspondence is from quarterly or annual letters. This is especially true if you have an account smaller than one hundred thousand dollars. M. G. spoke with his clients at least once every quarter, no matter how small they were. He said that those small ones, while not making him much, sometimes would be the contacts that would bring in the larger ones.

There are some things that people just take for granted, attitudes or rules that we just accept because "that's just how it's done." How many people would have a problem when asked whether their current advisor cares enough about their account to stay in contact like M. G. does? How many customers would all of a sudden feel slighted by this customer service?

He has set his strategy in motion, and just like the English did to the Spanish, it's a move that his large competitors aren't prepared to follow. For M. G., with fewer than one hundred clients, it takes him a week tops to contact them and discuss their accounts, regardless of what size they are. For one of the "big boys" to match his promise, with their hundreds or thousands of accounts, they would have to hire another complete staff to make it happen. Their guns aren't going to shoot that far. M. G. is a small blip on their radar. He wouldn't be worth the effort or expense of hiring one hundred more employees. While they will probably incorporate his philosophy slowly if he is starting to hurt them financially, by then it will be too late and M.G. will be one of the big boys.

To date the small company that M.G. started is growing at a phenomenal rate and to this day, he still calls each client at least once a quarter to discuss how they are doing. His small company was willing to be the solution for a problem that most of his current clients didn't even know they had. He was willing to make promises that the big boys couldn't keep, a promise he couldn't have made if he was as large as his competitors.

Action Summary:

- ■ Are there things that customers complain about in your industry that they just accept?
- ■ Can you make a business change that could solve this problem?
- ■ Find out what your competitors' size keeps them from doing.
- ■ Are they too small or too large to make moves that your company could?

U-Haul Superiority

Consumer truck rental business is one of the hardest kinds of business to start. Operating margin is less than 3% across the industry. Strong companies have gone bankrupt by trying to serve the consumer rental business. Ryder, one of the biggest consumer truck rental companies and the only worthy competitor of U-Haul, sold off its fleet of trucks in 1996! But yet, U-Haul has managed to thrive in the industry. While everyone was struggling and no one in the industry had more than a 3% profit margin, U-Haul had an amazing 10% margin! How did U-Haul manage the coup?

Unlike its competitors, U-Haul looked past its core truck renting business. U-Haul figured that people's moving process began with renting a truck. But it didn't end there. After renting a truck, people would look for other services like insurance, temporary storage space, rentals of trailers, packing boxes and various other accessories and while customers shop for the lowest rate for truck rentals, once the truck rental agreement has been signed, they stop price shopping and pay retail prices for other accessories.

Once U-Haul figured this out, it started renting its trucks at break-even cost. It made the trucks a "loss leader" and made all the money on selling products after the truck has been rented! Because U-Haul found virtually no competitors in the accessories business, it could easily sell them at high margins. As a result, U-Haul thrived in a dead industry, enjoying 10% margins!

Action Summary:

- ■ Ask yourself: Why do people buy my products?
- ■ What else could you sell to people to help them in their cause?
- ■ Test selling an in-demand product for a loss if it leads to people buying the rest of your products (Groceries do this all the time selling milk at a loss just because it gets people into the store who end up buying more products).

The 24-hour Checkout

Hotels are very rigid in their time schedules. They don't think in terms of their customers' convenience. They tell you when to check in and when to check out. In most hotels, if you stay 30 minutes more than their checkout time, they will charge you for one whole day!

Mr. Baxter decided to change that in his Sheraton hotel. To improve the hotel services, he decided to offer a 24-hour checkout facility. It took him 6 months and lots of work to put the idea into practice. He had to juggle time schedules, make some changes in certain procedures and convince the managers and workers to go along with the idea. His hard work paid off. When competitors' hotels were only 66% full, Mr. Baxter's Sheraton boasted a record 90% occupancy rate!

Action Summary:

- Do more for your clients than is required by the industry standards.
- Try to remove procedures that are inconvenient for your clients.
- Give them more flexibility.
- How can you provide better service?
- How can you improve the experience your clients receive?

Technique: Vilify

I know you ain't talking about my momma!

So we are trying to change people's perceptions without boring them with statistics (that they would ignore anyway), and without lying to them (which would catch up with you in the end). Give the audience just enough information and the right information to let them come to their own conclusions. In the consumers' mind we plant a seed, a seed of growth about one company or a seed of doubt about another.

Here is an example. How many people are familiar with PABA? Some of you may be, so please don't discount my example here if you find that you are one of the "chosen few." I am not sure what PABA is, nor have I ever really had the desire to go and research it. My sunscreen is "PABA Free" though. Now, without ever doing any research or knowing anything about PABA, I know that if I ran into a dramatic showdown between purchasing two different sunscreens, one with PABA and one without, I would choose PABA free. The reason: They went out of their way to tell me that they were "PABA Free" on the label. You don't see any brands announcing that they now have "PABA" so it must be bad. It probably is, but the point is that most consumers don't know.

Hypothetically, what if PABA is a moisturizer that is completely harmless and your company was called "PABAscreen Sun Block"? You would currently be either out of business, or in the middle of spending an exorbitant amount of money and time trying to quickly re-educate the public on the benefits of your product, all because your competitor vilified PABA by stating that they were free of it. No one ever claims to be free of something if it is good, right? And they never told you it was bad, just that they were free of it.

Here is a "real world" example of "Vilify". There was a commercial about cleaning carpets in my hometown. A company that used dry chemicals to clean the carpets created the commercial. The last line of their commercial was "We guarantee, no steam will touch your carpet." My carpets were just steam cleaned by a competing carpet company not a day before I heard that message. My concern was what their steam had done to my carpet. I called the sales manager who was a friend of mine and asked him what his steam was going to do to my carpet. He said, "85% of carpet companies recommend steam because you don't want to leave chemicals on the carpet." He then went into a discussion about carpet being made of plastic or something and how steam is what is best. I didn't really care once he let me know that steam isn't going to cause my carpet to shrink in from the walls. My big fear of walking in and having an area rug where I once had wall-to-wall was gone.

How many people didn't know the sales manager well enough to call and find out for themselves if steam was bad? Then I paused; no one ever said steam was bad. His competitor didn't even say steam was bad. How then did I go from being happy a day before with my steamed carpets, to on the edge of having to choke a sales manager out because of my fears of a shrinking room? With one simple line, "We guarantee no steam," his competitor vilified steam.

This could be devastating to the company I used because they had "steam" in the title. If this continued off the radar, it could spell disaster. I went back to this company and warned them that by either great planning or "dumb luck" their competitor had thrown a curve into their marketing that was going to be the Paris' arrow to their Achilles' heel. This company's strength was their high-priced steam equipment. Their competitor used the vilify technique to turn a strength into a perceived weakness.

They chose to continue with their normal advertising plan. After all, I was just a local marketing guy. You have to get off of an airplane to be an expert.

To this day, I don't really know which is better for your carpet. But I do know that the dry chemical company didn't have the same difficulty getting clients during the same time period. Was this loss of business due to people just not getting their carpets cleaned all of a sudden or was it because a large market of people mistakenly assumed steam is bad for their carpets and didn't care enough to ask?

Pure

Even in the 19th century, the beer industry was as competitive as it is today and Schlitz beer was at the bottom of the fierce competition. It was no. 5. The beer companies spent thousands of dollars advertising their brands. Schlitz bought full-page ads in leading newspapers with just one word on the page: PURE. They thought that by SCREAMING about their top quality beers, they would beat their competition in sales! But all the money spent on advertising was just going down the drain. Thousands of dollars spent on advertising campaigns did not increase sales and Schlitz beer could not sell more as even other beer brands were spending on advertising like crazy! They knew they had to change something. So they hired Claude Hopkins. Claude Hopkins wanted to know how beer was made. So he went on a factory tour and what he found amazed him:

- *Only water from 4,000-foot deep artesian wells was used to ensure that the water was the cleanest it could be.*
- *Beer was made only from original yeast cell that were developed after 1,200 experiments on mother yeast cells.*
- *Beer was dripping over pipes in plate-glass rooms filled with filtered air so that the beer could be cooled without any impurities.*
- *Every pump and pipe was cleaned twice a day. Every bottle was sterilized four times before beer was poured into it.*

When Claude Hopkins asked why the public wasn't educated about this process, he was told, "Because all the other beer producers do it the same way." And Hopkins replied, "Yes, but nobody has ever told the story." Hopkins created an ad campaign that actually educated the public on how Schlitz beer was manufactured and how pure it really was. His ads showed the steps taken to create "Pure" beer. His campaign took Schlitz beer from the no. 5 position to no. 1!

Action Summary:

- Educate the public. Educate your clients.
- Tell them how your product is made. Answer the what, where, when, how and why.
- Be the first to claim something good, even if it's typical in the industry; the customers may not know.
- Claude vilified not being Pure, when he claimed that Schlitz was.
- Customers just assumed that since they were claiming it, their competition must not be.

Sneaky Cold Calling

Andy is a graphic designer who designs logos and illustrations for companies. Andy used to use cold calling to earn some business. But the National Do-Not-Call-list initiated by the FTC in the United States meant that telemarketers could no longer cold call to people who were on the list after January 1, 2005. Even though the do-not-call list doesn't cover business-to-business cold calls, many business owners would become angry and complain when Andy called them. So Andy decided to do something to not anger people. He found a solution to get around the problem.

He started calling businesses after their regular working hours so that he could reach their voice mail systems. Andy would then leave a voice message that he had prepared beforehand, which gives a few benefits of hiring Andy. The voice message is timed to end before the voice mail time ends and the voice message gives a call to action to the business owner to call Andy back. By not disturbing people during their working hours, Andy doesn't anger them and the results are good too. About 40% of people who listen to his voice mail call Andy the next day and most of them commend him for not wasting their time with cold calls during regular working hours!

Action Summary:

- This is a sneaky tactic and not everyone should use it. Business owners can still become angry about this cold calling tactic. But most of them won't mind, as you are not disturbing them when they are busy.
- Andy vilified interruptions by going out of his way not to do it. The people who call you back will be much more receptive to listening about the services you offer.
- If you do use this tactic, make sure that your voice message is short, personal, and asks people to call you back the next day if they are interested in your offer.

The DVD Market

Unlike the developed nations, in India, the DVD market isn't as mature. VHS format is still widely used. Video rental stores have to carry both DVD and VHS of all the movies and documentaries and other videos to rent out. Half the population doesn't have DVD players and the other half has thrown away their VHS players. One video rental store saw that it had to carry double the inventory because of this problem and it planned to cater to people who own DVD players. But they didn't want to just tell half of their clients to buzz off. So they decided to convert all of their clients into DVD renters.

They bought generic DVD players at wholesale value. Each DVD player cost them Rupees (Rs.) 2995. These DVD players cost Rs.9000 in the retail market. The rental store then started discounting the DVD players by 33% and started selling them in their stores. "DVD Players for Rs.6000" attracted a lot of folks. But then they went one step further. They offered a limited time bonus of "50 free DVD rentals" with the purchase of the DVD player. Fifty rentals would otherwise bring in Rs.2500 (at Rs.50 per rental). In essence, they received Rs.6000 for providing goods worth Rs.5495 and they built a loyal client base – by providing them 50 free rentals! They converted hundreds of people who rented VHS to start renting DVDs (and reduced their inventory costs). They made a handsome profit in return.

Action Summary:

- If you provide a service that is dependent on another product, buy that product at wholesale value and then offer a bundled package with that product and your service together. (You could also joint venture with the product seller to bundle both products together. This way, you won't even
- have to invest in inventory.)
- Provide bonuses to sweeten the deal. Provide a bonus that people keep on receiving for quite some time and they are more

likely to become loyal to you.

■ Vilify the competitors who aren't supplying the dependent product. "We want to make sure you have the newest technology at a reasonable rate."

Positioning
"Compared to you, I'm freaking Albert Einstein"

When it comes to a new product or procedure, the challenge is that of overcoming the incumbent, the tried and true battle-tested original. You must convince the consumer that your product is either new or improved. I never understood how a product could be both new and improved. If it's new, how do you improve it? And if it's improved, it can't be new as there would be nothing to improve. Figure out which one you are, and find something in the market to compare yourself to. If you are coming into the market against an old competitor then you might try to position yourself as the new thing by creating a time line.

"My grandfather always told me he shaved with a straight edge razor, sharpened on a stone every morning. He said my dad was lucky to get one of those newfangled hand razors with the blade already angled for you. I remember how he ridiculed my older brother for being a pansy with his Mach III razor. I don't think I'm gonna tell him about my NEW OCHO CALIENTE. Eight blades to ensure I get down to 'a few less layers of skin' smooth. It comes with two strips, one moisture strip to ensure a quick shave, and one absorbent one to help the blood clot quickly. Now that's sharp!"

This is a joke that points out the technique but it is true. Invention is the mother of necessity. Now you probably think that sounds backwards but it isn't. You can argue that necessity is the mother of invention but did we need the Mach III or the Quattro? Remember shaving just fine with a two-bladed razor? How about camera cell phones? Radios in the shower? CD alarm clocks? Microwave? They may be faster, cheaper, brighter, neater, but rarely are they necessary for existence (I might now argue for the microwave or the air conditioner, 'cause I believe I might starve and overheat…but I digress). But the marketing makes them seem so necessary that you have to have one. If your razor doesn't have multiple blades with moisturizing strips, you might as well be a grandfather with his stone-sharpened straight edge. What's wrong with you?

To defeat something that has long dominated a category, you must position it as the old and your product or service as the new way of doing things. You might not catch all the audiences as many still use their double blade-razor, but you will have the competition jumping trying to save market share.

Selling Rocks

L. G. had no real talent. He was not strong enough to do manual work. He was not skilled in any job or profession. The only thing working for him was his imagination. He was a great creative thinker and with his imagination, he sold more than 60,000 ordinary rocks! How can you sell rocks to people? How can you persuade people to buy ordinary rocks that can be picked up for free? By repackaging them, of course, and that's what L. G. did.

L. G. painted the rocks pink and then he created a booklet that advertised the ordinary rocks as "pets." The booklet talked about a pet that requires no license, will not reproduce, will protect the owner from attacks and it comes in a pretty pink color. The booklet was named "Care and Training of Your Pink Pet Rock." It went on to talk about how the pet was amazing for security and required low maintenance. The pet rocks require no lessons to sit, play dead or roll over. For defense, the owners could take the pet rock out of their pockets and throw them at intruders.

The pink pet rocks sold like crazy. L. G. sold more than

60,000 rocks from gift shops. The pink pet rock was considered so cool that people actually paid a premium price on them! L. G. built a small fortune by re-packaging and selling ordinary rocks found on beaches for free!

Action Summary:

- Even a worthless item can be sold for a lot of money when it's repackaged.
- Position the product as something different than what most people think of when they see it. Positioning it uniquely has power.
- Simple repackaging can enhance the value of a product. It can convert a commodity product into a specialty one and then you can charge a premium on it.
- Some simple ways of re-packaging are changing the color, adding a twist, or weaving a story around the product.

Parker Pen Rumblings

George Safford Parker was a schoolteacher in the 1880s and 1890s. Getting fed up with the unreliable ink pens that were available in the market then, he decides to make his own pens for his students. He patents his technique in December of 1889 and soon forms the Parker Pen Company with another partner. Within 18 months, he makes 2 more types of pens and has moderate success selling them. In 1894, he hits the jackpot with his 4th model - "the lucky curve" pen. During the next century, the Parker Pen Company sees everything: from 2 world wars to the Great Depression. But they still show stellar growth year after year. New pens are invented constantly, even after George Parker's death. The company sells its pens in all corners of the world. Parker Pen Company builds a fine distribution system over the years. In the 1980s, the pens are available everywhere. They are available on racks in all kinds of stores: from grocery stores to drug stores and even in discount stores. But trouble seems to be right around the corner.

On February 1, 1986, a few old executives get together and buy the entire company in a leveraged buyout and make Parker Pens a privately held-company. They don't like the image Parker Pens is forming and they change the entire selling strategy. They throw the entire distribution system out! By the end of 1986, their bottom line is blood red! The balance sheet shows a year-end loss of half a million dollars! But the executives don't look worried. They think their new plan will work and they'll be rich soon. Their new marketing plan increases demand by curtailing supply of the pens. The pen is no longer sold anywhere and everywhere. It's only sold in high-end stores like jewelry shops and office supply stores, and only under glass in nice packaging, not on any racks out in the open. The price of the pens is increased too. The critics cry, but the plan seems to work. The year the executives buy Parker Pens, it makes a loss of $500,000. A year after that, it makes a stellar profit of $23.4 million!

Action Summary:

- ■ Parker Pens is positioned as a luxurious brand of pen and sometimes even used as jewelry because of its higher demand and lower supply.
- ■ One way of increasing demand (and increasing positioning) is by supplying your product in limited quantity. You can sell fewer products and yet make more profits by curtailing supply and increasing prices.

- The company didn't only curtail supply; they also improved the perception of the pens by selling them only in higher-end stores in nice packaging.
- Improve your packaging and you can charge a higher price too.

Selling Unwanted Paintings

A gallery owner had just had a very nice year. He had featured some very talented painters the past year and had sold most of the paintings showcased in his gallery. Only a few still troubled him. The gallery owner hadn't been able to sell these 3 paintings in the entire year. It wasn't that the 3 paintings were ugly. In fact they were extremely beautiful and had won some critical acclaim too. But the public was hesitating in paying the high prices that the gallery owner was asking for them. It seemed like the gallery owner would have to budge and reduce the prices on these 3 un-sellable paintings. But instead of reducing the prices on these 3 paintings, the gallery owner did something quite different. He commissioned an upcoming painter to paint a painting on a larger canvas – as large as 2 normal paintings together. The huge painting was exquisite, with beautiful use of design and colors. The gallery owner priced this painting at an insanely high rate. Even though the painting was beautiful, no one in his or her right mind would pay that much for it. The gallery owner then placed that huge painting next to one of the un-sellable paintings and lo! Within a week, the previously un-sellable painting was sold. The gallery owner then placed that huge painting next to the other un-sellable painting. The outcome was the same. Within 3 weeks, the gallery owner had sold 3 previously un-sellable products without reducing the prices.

Action Summary:

- If you don't have something that will help position your product, create it.

- This is the power of comparison at work. When people would saw the huge painting, they loved it. But seeing the high price, they would hesitate. Then their eyes would fall on the painting next to it, and they would end up buying that painting – as it now looked much more affordable in comparison.

- Come up with an "Extra Large" version of your product and price it insanely high. Most people won't buy it. But the comparison tactic would then kick in and make those people consider buying your other products.

- In place of extra large, your product could also be extra small, or extra thin. Just make it unique.

Real Estate Magnet

Real estate is a fiercely-competitive industry. Dozens of realtors crop up when the economy is good and real estate prices are high. It is hard to stand out from the crowd when you do the same thing that other realtors do: sell houses. One realtor in South Beach named Marie used a tactic successfully that helped her leave her competition lagging way behind.

Marie wrote an 80-page book that described the various neighborhoods in Miami Beach. She added some real estate sales data that showed how hot South Beach real estate was and she gave an enticing name to the book: "The Secrets of South Beach Real Estate." She repackaged the data available in any realtor's office and made it into a book and she used this book as a lead generation tool. Marie tried to position herself as the local real estate guru.

This alone would have gotten Marie new business. But she went one step further and used one more tactic that got loads of business coming her way. Marie started selling the book in tourist places. She started targeting out-of-town tourists. She placed her books in unusual places like behind the counters in restaurants.

Marie realized that many tourists would be curious about buying a house in Miami after having experienced the wonderful atmosphere there. So she placed the books in places where people make buying decisions on impulse. The tourists would read her book and get interested in buying a house, either as a vacation place or a retirement place, and they would call up Marie for more information. Thus, Marie ended up selling expensive condos and houses at high prices to a target audience no one else went after.

Action Summary:

- Writing a book or a report is a great way to improve your credibility.
- You can position yourself as the expert by writing an informational product.
- The informational product will work as a magnet for you, attracting new customers.
- Focus on a target audience that no one else goes after. Marie not only sold tons of her books, she also sold dozens of houses because she went after the tourists instead of the locals.

Marketing with Music

Psychologist Adrian North was curious about the role music played in affecting people's emotions. He got together with researchers at Britain's Universities of Leicester and Surrey to run a scientific musical experiment. The research group persuaded James Davis, the proprietor of Softley's restaurant, to take part in their experiment. They played classical music, pop music or no music over the course of 18 days in the restaurant and they tracked the average amount each diner paid. They tracked money spent over starters, main course, dessert, coffee, wine and other bar drinks, and the overall bill amount. The results were amazing. They found that on average, each diner spent:

- *$35.00 when no music was played*
- *$36.75 when pop music was played*
- *$40.00 when classical music was played*

Classical music increased the amount of money people spent by $5 per diner! According to Adrian North, classical music increases spending owing to its "connotations of affluence, sophistication and wealth. When people feel more cultured and sophisticated they are more likely to spend money on items they think cultured and sophisticated people would order." Thinking conservatively, Softley's restaurant will increase their revenue by $150,000 per year – all just for playing classical music!

Action Summary:

- Music affects your ambience. It affects what people think about your place.
- Playing classical or soft music positions your establishment as classy.
- Classy environments cause people to spend more money than they would in a less fancy environment.
- Could you change up music, decorations, lighting or employee

dress to class up your establishment? You could end up making more money.

Campus Tour Guides

Michigan Technological University (MTU) is a fine university with some very fine programs and they get more students to apply with them than they can accommodate. MTU started receiving lots more inquiries from students to take a university tour. When the load got to be too much, Bill Roberts, who coordinates the campus visit program, suggested that MTU start charging people who wanted a tour guide. Something weird happened. The number of people who came for a tour guide did decrease. But the number of people who applied to become a student at MTU actually increased! Of the people who took the tour, 99% applied to become a student and of those who were accepted, 90% decided to actually attend MTU.

That's quite a lot, taking into consideration that an average high school student applies to at least 4 universities! By charging for the campus tour guides, MTU attracted more qualified people and once these people actually paid a small fee for the tour guide, they had to be consistent and spend a bit more to apply to become a student too.

Action Summary:

- Demonstrate your product and get people to actually try your product, and they will purchase.
- By charging for the tours, the school was positioned as more valuable.
- Start charging a small fee for a demonstration, and you will

attract fewer but more qualified people and you will end up selling more, too.

Intimidating Through a Brochure

Robert Ringer is a millionaire real estate broker today. But he wasn't always so successful. In his book "Winning Through Intimidation," Robert tells about how he got past the gatekeepers into the property owner's office. When Robert Ringer started out as a real estate broker, he had no connections, no rich relatives, and no big success stories behind him. No property owner would take him seriously when he approached them asking if they were interested in selling their property. Most of the time, when Ringer called their offices to set up an appointment to make his presentation, he didn't even get past the gatekeepers.

Ringer invested some of his money in building his "image" up. He created a brochure that cost an insane amount of $5 per copy! The brochure had a glossy black cover so rich that no one could resist opening it. The first page started with the words:

"Earth To Life...Support To The Explorer...A Base To The Wise... An Investment"

The brochure then went on to say how Ringer could help get a very good price for the property. Ringer then mailed the black brochure to property owners' offices through first class mail a few days before he called them up! This time around, however, the gatekeepers didn't slam the phone down. Instead, Ringer was automatically connected to the boss who was eager to hear more about how Ringer could help him get top dollar for the property!

In Robert Ringer's own words: "The brochure was specifically created to accomplish two objectives: the first was to eliminate the question of who I was; the second was to make it almost impossible for an owner to forget me."

Action Summary:

- ■ The easiest way to get past the gatekeeper is to send something out of the ordinary to the office. If you send something unique, the gatekeeper will be forced to pass it on to the boss, who will then remember you when you call on him.
- ■ Invest in building your "image" up.
- ■ Invest in making a good first impression. Send glossy brochures before calling the prospective clients.

Good Booking Club

Trends show men aged 18-25 are getting richer and richer every day. Penguin Books, a publisher in the UK, wanted a piece of this rich pie. But they found it really hard to sell books to this market. Young men under 25 tended to spend all their money on cars, football and video games. They showed no interest in buying and reading books. Penguin Books was looking for a hook, a story with which they could entice young men to read and one landed right in their laps when relationship expert Tracy Cox was quoted as saying:

"It takes less than a minute to decide if you fancy someone, so it's essential you can flirt suggestively and strike up a conversation. Finding a common interest is crucial and carrying a good book can often help break the ice and gives you both something to talk about."

Taking the initiative, Penguin asked NOP to run an independent survey asking women if they preferred men who read books or men who don't read books. As predicted, the survey found that 78% of women think men who read are likely to be much better in bed (*Survey said NOTHING about men who wrote books though-dang it).

That was all Penguin Books needed. They then started a "Good Booking" book of the month club and sent press releases to the media revealing the survey results. The media jumped at the story and gave a lot of ink to the survey results and the "Good Booking" club.

This did help in selling more books to young men aged 25 and below. But soon the story got old and the press stopped writing about it. This is when Penguin got the bright idea to leverage the promotional campaign for the book of the month club with a contest. The contest was simple. Penguin sent a stunning model to a random bookstore in the UK once a month. She picked one man under 25 and gave him £1000 cash. The only condition was that man has to be reading that month's Good Booking book of the month. After selecting the lucky male winner, Penguin took pictures of the model and the man together (featuring the man with the book in his hand) and sent it to media channels every month and month after month, they gave the media an opportunity to write about the survey results and feature the Good Booking book club. Penguin managed to make an old story seem new with the help of a contest and as a result, they got lots of free publicity every month for a £1000 contest.

Action Summary:

- Keep your eyes and ears open for a chance opportunity of an expert saying something good about your industry or even your company.

- Send press releases to media with an interesting story or survey and receive free publicity.
- Hold a monthly contest through which one person can receive a gift each month for buying your product. The gift doesn't have to be as expensive as £1000. It could be as inexpensive as a movie for two. Send press releases to the local media with photos of the winner and receive even more free publicity.
- To tap into a new market, let the winner of the contest be someone from that market.

The Rich Young Entrepreneur

Some years ago, a young 12-year-old kid named Michael in Houston wanted to earn some extra pocket money. He decided to become a paperboy. He went down to the distributor where he was given a bundle of papers and a list of randomly selected names of people who didn't have a subscription to the paper yet. The people were scattered all over the city.

Young Michael's job was to get the people on this list to become subscribers. He did manage to get a few subscribers here and there, but nothing to boast about. Soon, he saw a pattern emerging: There were two categories of people who were much more likely to buy a subscription to a newspaper than anyone else:

1. People who had just moved to a new house

2. People who had just married

These people's lives had just gone through a major overhaul and thus they were most keen on buying goods and services including newspaper subscriptions. Once Michael discovered the pattern, he started thinking of ways through which he could contact these people and these people only. He asked around and he did receive an answer: the local courthouse.

Michael then hired a small army of other 12-year-old kids to go to the local courthouse every day to find out the contact information for everyone who had just purchased a new house and who had applied for a marriage license.

Michael then spent all his time and energy selling the subscriptions to these people who were more prone to buy. His list of potential buyers had gotten smaller, but his number of sales had increased. He was making more sales than people who were three times his age!

By the time summer was over, Michael was earning more in commission than his school teachers were making!

Today Michael is quite wealthy. He became rich because he learned the lesson early in his life: to sell to a targeted segment market.

Action Summary:

- Don't try to be all things to everybody. Focus on a target audience that is most likely to buy your products.
- After you win one market segment, you can move on to the next one.

Enlightenment Near the Elevator

The building was tall. I was on the ground floor though, waiting for the elevator to come and take me up and what I saw while waiting turned on some lights in my brain.

A lady in a business suit turned up from nowhere. She went over to a vending machine and of all things; she purchased a bottle of water. This wasn't enlightening in itself. But when you take the whole ground floor into account, it is a bit surprising. You see, there was a cold water cooler right across from the vending machine. It would have just taken the lady three steps to cross over and drink water for free. Yet she spent $1.25 on a bottle of water.

Why? Why did the lady buy the bottle of water when she could drink it for free? The answer is perception. It is perceived that bottled water is safer than tap water. It is, however, not so. According to some studies, tap water contains some minerals that even bottled mineral water doesn't and these are minerals that the body needs.

Did you know that bottled water costs more than gas?

It is interesting how perception makes people spend more money on things. Water is available for free almost everywhere. Yet bottled water is big business. Interesting tidbit: A gallon of bottled water is more expensive than a gallon of gas! And that's not in the deserts in Asia where oil is abundant and water scarce! While gas is $2.70 a gallon, mineral water would cost $5.00 per gallon and tap water is available for free. Packaging and perception make all the difference.

Action Summary:

- How do your clients perceive your product?
- Improving the perception is easy. By changing the packaging, the perception changes too.
- Water is free. Yet bottled water is not. Oxygen is free. Yet people pay money to breathe it in oxygen bars. Just re-package your product and people will be willing to pay more for it.
- It's all in the perception. A book can be sold as a course pack for more money. Free advice can be sold for profit as consultation.

Ten-Minute Ice Cream Vacation

Americans are growing fatter every day. More people are dieting and exercising these days. Atkins, South Beach and the latest diets are always in the news. The food chains are even shaping up. McDonald's dumped their Super Size meals. Other fast food chains are coming out with salads. Ice cream parlors like Baskin-Robbins are coming up with non-fat ice creams and yogurts.

And yet, one ice cream parlor is not heeding the mainstream media's advice. While most food product companies and restaurants are going low-carb, Cold Stone is selling rich, creamy ice creams that have tons of calories and it's succeeding.

A typical ice cream in Cold Stone will have nuts, fruits, candy, chocolate, fudge and even cake batter. Cold Stone's smallest cup is as big as Baskin-Robbins' large scoop! And Cold Stone sells even bigger ice cream scoops. The small, medium and large cups are called "like it", "love it" and "gotta have it."

Kevin Donnellan, senior public relations manager for Cold Stone Creamery says, "We are super premium ice cream. We like to think that when people are on the Atkin's [Diet] or South Beach Diet, if they want to cheat, they're going to go to Cold Stone Creamery because they want the best...It's really the ice cream lovers who want to take that ten-minute vacation and really indulge and enjoy themselves."

Cold Stone sells luxury. People get to eat the best ice creams and they even pay accordingly. A small cup at Cold Stone costs as much as $3! And yet people can't have enough of it.

Because Cold Stone is doing what others aren't, it's growing rapidly. In 1999, there were 74 Cold Stone parlors. Today there are over 900!

Action Summary:

- Do what others aren't doing. Be different from your competition and you will grow faster.
- Target a specific market. While other ice cream parlors targeted kids, Cold Stone targeted women aged between 18 and 34.
- Sell an experience. Sell luxury. If you make the best quality products, people will pay more for them.

The Six-Dollar Burger

In the fall of 1960, Wilbur Hardee opened a drive-in quick service restaurant. The restaurant became extremely well known and in 1963, it became the first in the fast food industry to make a public offering of stock - two years before McDonald's!

Sometime after that, Hardee's got lost in the shuffle. It could not keep up with McDonald's, Burger King, Wendy's and other fast food chains cropping up everywhere. Hardee's was losing a lot of money. The big chains were introducing $1 menus and Hardee's, like many other restaurants, tried to keep up with them. This strategy almost ran them out of business. Things were turning from bad to worse until someone in management made some important key decisions.

While the big chains were cutting down costs and spending millions in advertising to attract more people, Hardee's started increasing their prices. They decided to focus on earning more per diner than on bringing more diners in. Instead of waging a price war and coming out with their own $1 menu, Hardee's introduced the Carl's Jr. "six dollar burger." They made the burger thick. They used pure Angus beef. They became well known for thick and tasty burgers that tasted as good as homemade ones.

They started doing what no other hamburger joint was willing to do. They invested in making quality burgers when others were cutting costs. They started selling more expensive burgers when others were introducing cheap ones and Hardee's prospered. They grew. Today they have about 4,000 restaurant joints all over the world! Oh, and they sell the "six dollar burgers" for only $3.99.

Action Summary:

- When the competition is fierce, focus on their weakest attributes. Do something different.
- 4,000 people x $1 = $4,000 revenue and also 1,000 people x $4 = $4,000 revenue. You can earn more by charging high prices even though the total number of buyers is low.
- Letting people believe that they are receiving a deal will make them buy more as well as increase their satisfaction. Hardee's used a superb tactic by charging just $4 for the "six dollar burger."
- You too can make use of the tactic: show that your product is worth more and then give a deal to win more clients.

Ringing Earrings

E. Joseph Cossman was a master seller. He sold more than 35 million dollars worth of products through mail order, and this was half a century ago. He then went on to write a book on how he did it all. It was known that Joseph Cossman only sold products on one condition: that he received exclusive rights to sell them in a specific region.

One day, a man came to Joseph and told him he couldn't sell his earrings and make a profit. He gave Joseph Cossman exclusive rights to sell them.

The earrings had little bells attached to them. No earrings like those were available on the market. Joseph took on the rights.

But he soon found out that having a novel product does not necessarily mean that people will buy it. He was having trouble selling the earrings too. The earrings were just not sellable through mail order.

But Joseph Cossman didn't give up. He put on his creative cap and starting thinking. He renamed the product. He called them "mothers-in-law earrings." He weaved a story around the earrings, how they could be gifted to mothers-in-law and they would notify the person if his mother-in-law was nearby. As the earrings had bells, they would ring when the mothers-in-law walked!

Joseph Cossman then targeted newly-wed grooms instead of women. He made a small fortune selling the earrings through mail order. He managed to convert a mail order loser into a big winner.

Action Summary:

- ■ Select a target audience. Joseph Cossman selected newly-wed grooms.
- ■ Give a killer name to your product. A good name can mean the difference between profit and loss.
- ■ Weave a story. Storytelling sells.

Counter-Branding
Be the Yin to their Yang

Many categories are dominated by just one brand. This is usually recognizable when you can use the brand name as the generic name for the product. It's time to create a counter-brand. Roy Williams, the "Wizard of Ads" shares the example of this technique in one of his Monday Morning Memos. It's paraphrased below, talking about Starbucks. Notice how I didn't have to name the category? All I had to say was "Starbucks" and you knew we were talking about coffee. That's category dominance.

In the February 2005 issue of QSR magazine, Marilyn Odesser-Torpey writes about Coffee Wars, opening with the question, "Starbucks will certainly remain top dog among coffee purveyors, but who is next in line?" A little later we read, "Many of the competitors in the coffee segment are Starbucks look-alikes; if you take the store's signage down, it would be hard to tell the difference."

Traditional wisdom tells us to (1) study the leader, (2) figure out what they're doing right, (3) try to beat them at their own game.

Are all competitive coffee houses forever doomed to play folksy music to the yuppie laptop crowd sitting in utilitarian looking chairs under creamy colored neutral backdrops...all in the shadow of mighty Starbucks? Yes, until one of them launches a counter-brand.

Counter-branding isn't easy to do, and can be dangerous. But when you're dominated, it's a better option than copying the leader. If you mimic the leader, the best you can be is a good copy of number one.

The steps in counter-branding are these:
1. **Figure out the characteristics of the monster brand.**
2. **Create a brand with exactly the opposite theme.**

3. Without using the brand name of your competitor, become the anti-them.

When you're up against an overwhelming competitor, you don't need to name them. Everyone knows who they are.

The characteristics of a Starbucks are:

1. **Atmosphere:** This is where the educated and important meet to remind themselves they are educated and important. Bring your laptop and log on to the Wi-Fi and work away. Join a conversation about interior design or socialism, and drink some coffee.
2. **Colors:** Muted, romantic colors. Every tone has black added.
3. **Sounds:** Eclectic music, folksy, soft and melodious.
4. **Lighting:** Shadowy, dim lighting…feeling almost sleepy.
5. **Pace:** Slow and ultra chilled. They aren't rushing anything, but then again, that isn't why you came.
6. **Names:** Distinctly Italian and uppity names. Sizes include 'Grande' and 'Venti' and the drinks include Caramel Macchiato and Lattes. (Your pronunciation will be wrong, and the "barista" will point it out. That is part of the job description. You cannot punch them!)

JoToGo is the counter-brand to Starbucks:

1. **Atmosphere:** High speed, rip-roaring ready to go. We are here for caffeine!
2. **Colors:** Primary colors that you wouldn't doze off to.
3. **Sounds:** Most likely a kickin' guitar rift and bad-ass drum solo somewhere.
4. **Lighting:** Future's so bright, got to wear shades.

5. **Pace:** It's like the guy making my coffee has been drinking coffee. Caffeine!!!
6. **Names:** Plain. Descriptive as opposed to uppity-sounding.

Here is how a counter brand commercial would sound:

Most people think that to get a fast cup of coffee you have to settle for fast-food coffee ...or worse...convenience store coffee, and to get a good cup of coffee you have to stand in line for 20 minutes at some snooty coffeehouse where things can't just be medium and large, but have to be "grande" and "venti"' At JoToGo we serve really good coffee, really fast. We're the original drive-thru espresso bar serving all your favorite premium coffee drinks at lightning speed. So when you're on the go, get a JoToGo. No snooty attitude here, just fabulous coffee fast.

Monster brands leave room at the opposite end of the spectrum for a counter brand. They have to because they are so dominantly known for their brand. When the opportunity arises, be the Yin to their Yang.

P.S. - **JoToGo** is a real company – franchising at a rapid rate.

Jomo Jazzes Up the Gas Stations

Jomo is Japan's sixth-largest gas station chain with just over 4,000 gas stations and a healthy 10.4% market share. But they might not remain the sixth largest for long. If they keep their focus and innovative approach, the top gas station chain might soon find itself being toppled by Jomo. Whereas most gas stations try to provide speedy service in order to move customers out quickly and service more customers, Jomo does the opposite. Jomo tries to make their customers stay at the gas stations for as long as possible. In an article in Business 2.0 magazine, Yuihito Fujita of Jomo is quoted as saying: "Our objective is to make hanging around more fun."

To fulfill the objective, Jomo hires a top restaurant designer from Tokyo to jazz up the gas stations. In a test, 8 gas stations are renovated at a cost of $46,000 per station. Each station receives:

1. *Classy pumps*

2. *A café*

3. *Massage chairs*

4. *Kiddies' areas*

Everything is designed to make people spend more time at the gas stations and Jomo tops it off with their famous car wash dances. "Two men in blue outfits gyrate around a vehicle, slicing hoses through the air like samurai swords. They towel off the car, their movements perfectly choreographed. Customers watching from behind a glass wall sometimes applaud."

This upscale atmosphere entertains customers and makes them loyal to Jomo due to the experience they receive over there. The new stations attract more customers. Plus, it attracts rich and affluent customers who own expensive cars, and spend more on maintenance and repair. These new gas stations are a huge success already attracting 22% more vehicles per month. Sales are up by 15% and even better, per station operating profits are up by a whopping 82%.

The renovations are so successful that Jomo plans to roll out similar services to 2,000 of its gas stations within 3 years!

Action Summary:

- Sell an experience to people and they will become loyal customers.
- Position yourself as quality.
- Improve the atmosphere of your workplace and you'll attract a better audience.

■ A slight increase in sales leads to a huge increase in profits. Make people spend more time at your store and they'll buy more. This will lead to an increase in sales and an even higher increase in profits.

The environment is constantly changing in the battle for the consumer. Business owners must be careful if they are going to base their advertising on a competitor. A business must have reasons why it is strong, not just why its competitor is weak. There are always dangers when going on the attack, because, once a fight is started, it's hard to end it. And, as the Triangle of Destruction showed, for every strength that one business has, it inherently has a weakness tied to it.

The World of Business

Section Two

There were 5 monkeys in a large cage. In the middle of the cage was a ladder with some bananas hanging at the top. A monkey walked up the ladder and began to grab at the bananas. Instantly the monkeys were all hosed down with cold water. The next time the monkey went for the bananas, the same thing happened with the cold water. Pretty soon, the other monkeys wouldn't allow anyone near the bananas. They would physically attack them to prevent the cold water from the hose.

Soon, no monkeys would make a move towards the bananas. One monkey was taken out and replaced with a brand-new monkey that had never experienced the cold water. This new monkey received a beating when he went for the bananas. It didn't take long for him to realize that going after the bananas was bad. Another of the original monkeys was replaced with a new monkey and this process kept on repeating itself.

There reached a point that none of the original monkeys were in the cage, but still no one went for the bananas. At the end of the experiment, there was a cage full of monkeys that had never experienced the cold water, but yet no one would go near the bananas, because they would be attacked. It is just what they have always done.

This example demonstrates why I encourage business owners to be willing to break away from what everyone in their industry does when it comes to marketing. Very often "traditional wisdom" is neither traditional, nor wisdom. Sometimes we do things just because that is how it's always been done, but none of the original monkeys are around to tell us why.

Have you ever heard someone say, "That is how we've always done it!" when approached with a new way of doing something? (I used to answer, "Well, that doesn't mean it wasn't stupid when we started doing it," but it didn't make me really popular with upper management.) People who worry about the way things have always been done are going to stress over the "World of Business" ideas. The business strategies that will follow are the strategies that cause changes in the way YOU do business. A change like this brings risks, but as we all know, the greater the risk is, the greater the reward. Is there a way to methodically plan out changes in the function of a business and reduce the risk? Yes! The brainstorming technique is called "Business Topology."

Business Topology (Brain Storm)
"It's like déjà vu all over again!"

Realizing that there are rarely new problems that appear, it's safe to assume that somebody somewhere has had this problem. The only difference is it most likely was under different circumstances. Look for comparable business categories and try to find solutions for your problem that have already been tested. If the industry is a service industry, look at other businesses that do similar business transactions.

An example is Henry Ford. Before the assembly line, a single master engineer constructed the whole vehicle, from body to engine. That is why it took so long to make a vehicle, and why they cost so much. They were paying for someone with years of training in many different areas. Henry Ford was interested in producing mass quantities at a fraction of the cost. The assembly line, which is often credited to Henry Ford, was around before in a different industry. Henry toured a meat packing plant. On one end of the factory, a whole animal carcass would be wheeled in, and within a short period of time, packaged meat came out on the other end. By not using a "master butcher" and training a person to do a single cut, over and over, the factory could clear much more product than a single butcher would be able to and at a fraction of the cost.

So taking this "Business topology" from the meat packing industry to the automobile industry, Henry was able to mass-produce vehicles for the first time in history. It's ironic that Henry Ford's assembly line was a product of the meat packing industries' "dis-assembly" line.

So when a problem is facing a specific industry, it's worth taking a look outside of the usual places they get answers. Very often, it's not a new problem and it's already been solved. Looking at the other solutions to common problems can create an opportunity that was unseen before.

Listening Parties

Tonic Sol-Fa is a boy band with 4 members. They are different from the usual Backstreet Boys style. For one thing, they don't use any instruments in their songs. They are a true "a cappella" band using only the vocals in all their songs. For this reason, the big music producers consider them risky. Even though they make good music and people like them when they perform in bars and restaurants, no major music label was willing to sign them up. They performed close to 250 shows a year all over America with good success. Yet no major music label was willing to back them up. So they decided to release their music CD independently, on their own. The 4 band members knew that selling CDs would be hard without a major label's backing. So they started building a team of fans all over the nation from the very beginning, who could help spread the word. While deciding on the best way to build a buzz, band front man Shaun had an idea.

His mom used to hold Tupperware parties to sell Tupperware products to her friends and neighbors. Why couldn't the band copy the Tupperware marketing idea? Copy they did.

They sent pre-released CDs to 120 fans all over the nation and convinced these 120 fans to host "listening parties". They also sent a few banners and posters and free t-shirts and other memorabilia with which these fans could promote the band and the listening party and finally, they gave out order forms that the hosts could give away with which people could preorder their own CDs.

In no time, 120 people hosted 120 listening parties in dorm rooms and coffee shops and played the pre-released CDs all over the nation. Anywhere from 30 to 50 people attended each party and 50% of people who came to these parties ended up preordering their copies. To make it worth the host's time, Tonic Sol-Fa gave away a few gifts to the top performers who sold the highest number of CDs. The gift for the winning host was: a private live performance by the band at their place. The results of these listening parties were fabulous. The buzz created was phenomenal. People would talk about this band and their listening party for weeks after the party was over and besides the cost of giving away a few gifts, all the publicity they received was free!

Action Summary:

- ■ Throw a Tupperware style party for your product or service.
- ■ Equip your loyal clients and fans to spread the word about you. Show them how your product looks before it's released, so that they can talk about it.
- ■ Encourage them to host parties where they can showcase your product. If your product has a "demonstrable" quality, you can host Tupperware-type parties and sell your products!

Pool Yield Management

In 1999-2000, pool mania hit Bombay, India. New outlets with pool and snooker tables were popping up everywhere. Some streets would have as many as 4 pool outlets! Soon the market became oversaturated. Unfortunately, Shyam bought 6 pool tables and opened his own shop after the peak was over – while the pool craze was declining.

Shyam was a year too late and he soon found out that it wasn't as good a business as he'd thought. Shyam found that people would come to his shop and play pool and snooker over the weekends. But during the weekdays, his shop would be deserted. Shyam had to think of something to bring in people during the weekdays. He started thinking about who else had the same problem. He realized the hotel industry faced the same problem too. So he did some research to find out how the hotels dealt with the problem.

Shyam soon found that hotels used expensive software for "yield management." The software calculated the highest price at which a room could be rented out with maximum profit every day. As a result, they had different room rates on different days according to the season and the days. Shyam didn't have money to invest in such yield management software and besides, he didn't want to make things complicated for his regular clients and so, he thought of a simpler plan.

He printed out a few coupons. Each coupon was worth one game and the coupons could be redeemed only during weekdays and then Shyam started selling those coupons to the people who came to his shop over the weekend. He started selling the coupons for half the price of a regular game and as more people started buying those coupons, he increased their price to 2/3 the cost of a regular game. Shyam also gave bulk discounts if people bought more than 25 coupons together. As a result of his yield management technique, his pool shop became packed during weekdays too. Even though he discounted his prices, the enormous increase in volume more than doubled his profits.

As the pool shop got packed all the time, it soon became famous. It became a hangout spot for college students and soon, Shyam didn't need to sell his coupons for a discount anymore.

Action Summary:

- To solve a problem like Shyam's, look at how a hotel might take advantage of down time and customer loyalty.

■ Yield management is a good idea. Have different prices for different days or times. You could do this easily by copying Shyam's idea and selling coupons at a discount and making these coupons redeemable on certain days only.

Join the Club

Monica was complaining that during certain seasons, the business at her hair salon would die off. Her service is, after all, a luxury expense. If the money is there, the expense can be greater; if it isn't, then the profits are down. Using a similar business we did a quick topology experiment.

We came up with the movie rental business. Just like the hair business, clients use it when they have extra money. It has a short time window as far as actual time spent receiving the services and the movie rental industry has faced this problem for years. So she used the latest changes in the rental industry to solve the hair salon's problem.

Netflix and Blockbuster have the option of renting as many movies as you like during a month period, without late fees, by paying a monthly subscriber fee that is slightly greater than a the cost of a few new release rentals. Could a hair salon offer its services endlessly month in and month out for a membership fee as opposed to a service fee?

So if someone wanted a touchup, or an updo, they would merely have to make an appointment with one of the stylists and come in. No more money would exchange hands. Let's do the math:

i. Average stylists can see about 100 clients per month.

ii. The clients' average bill runs about $80 for a service.

iii. The appointment books are filled with holes, though.

iv. Stylists are averaging only 50 clients per month.

v. They pay booth rent of $100 per week, with 7 stylists.

vi. That is $2,800 profit for salon owner before expenses.

    1. With 500 memberships sold at $100 per month it would be $50,000 per month.

    2. You would need to have a minimum of 5 stylists, but let's use the current 7 on staff.

    3. Paying them each $5,000 per month, which increases their current incomes – cost $35,000.

    4. Profit to salon owner is $15,000 per month before expenses.

This is a perfect world scenario and there are challenges and problems to overcome, but it is an example of how to look at a membership with endless services to change your business. When first talking to Monica about this idea, I was met with "That's not how salons do business." To which I answered, "And that's why I think it might work."

Monica tried this technique on a very small scale. She only offered it to a sorority on the local university campus. It had really good results, enough results that opening it up to another sorority is in the plans. Sometimes, you must tip-toe into change because there is great fear in doing something new for many business owners and employees.

Action Summary:

- ■ Is your business model in a position that maybe a membership might help fill in those seasons when the business drops off?
- ■ Change is sometimes slow and many companies are afraid to step outside of their comfort zone.
- ■ Start with a smaller test group to see if an idea will work.
- ■ Remember you don't only have to change the company's method of doing business; you have to get customers to buy in also.

Carpet Cleaning Subscription

Paul ran a carpet cleaning company very successfully. He provided good services at an exceptionally low cost and over time, with good marketing and promotion, he turned his business into the most popular and profitable carpet cleaning business in the city. One of Paul's secrets was building a database. He enters each and every client's name in a dated database and sends each of them a letter to remind them to clean their carpets again every 6 months. This worked well. But yet, most of his clients bought carpet cleaning services only once in three years.

So one day, he sat down and wrote a 12-page report educating clients about how cleaning a carpet with the hot steam extraction process every 6 months would provide health benefits and why waiting longer than 6 months could be harmful for people's health. At the end of the report, he added an order form. If people said "yes" and filled out that form, he would go to their homes and clean their carpets every 6 months automatically.

He mailed this report to each of his clients and then gave them a call 3 days after they received the report. This led to 30% of his clients signing up for the 6-month automatic carpet cleaning "subscription" program. Within weeks, Paul doubled his profits and had to hire a lot more employees than he previously had.

Action Summary:

- Educate your clients. Tell them why your services will be beneficial to them, how they should use them, how often they should use them, etc.
- Don't assume that they know about it. Educate them.
- Build a database and send a reminder to your clients regularly.

- Start a subscription program wherein people can opt in to receive your services at regular intervals automatically. Once they say yes, you can go to their homes regularly without them having to call you and schedule an appointment.
- Use the two-step process for promoting your services. Send a letter and then follow up with a phone call.

Plumbing Insurance

Sunny was always good with his hands. Right after high school, he and two of his friends started a plumbing business. They struggled initially and broke up the partnership because of petty fights within 6 months, but Sunny continued on solo. He hit his groove when he got an idea: to go to bigger clients.

Instead of advertising and going to individual houses when they called him, Sunny started contacting bigger residential associations or office complexes and asked them if he could be their only plumber. Most refused him. But all of the complex managers kept Sunny in mind. They would often call up Sunny when a resident complained of a leak. Over the months, Sunny did become the exclusive plumber of a dozen big societies, but in an unofficial status. Then one day, Sunny got one more idea. Why not sell plumbing insurance to these societies and complexes?

Sunny approached these society managers once again and sold them on a plan: they pay him a monthly fee and if their residents have any problems day or night, weekday or weekend, Sunny would come and fix it within 4 hours (most of the time, sooner than that). According to the plan, the residents living in the society wouldn't have to pay astronomical plumbing prices to get a leak fixed. All they would have to pay for is parts and a very minimal labor fee.

In a short time, 10 associations agreed to hire Sunny after passing a resolution in their monthly meetings (for which Sunny showed up). All they did was add a fee on their residents' maintenance bill and then pay the amount to Sunny. Sunny went and roped in more office and residential complexes in his plan and after 3 months, he started working less, but because of his monthly plan, money kept on coming in like clockwork. He soon started earning a mid-six figure income without doing as much work as before.

Action Summary:

- An easy way to increase your income is to come up with a "warranty" or "insurance" program. Sell peace of mind.
- People can pay a yearly fee and in return you fix the widgets that you've sold to them when they break down.
- If you don't sell a product or service on which a warranty could be sold, you could come up with a subscription plan.
- People pay you now to consume or use your products later.
- Netflix.com changed the whole video rental game by asking people to pay now and then use later. You could do the same.

Joint Venture

"This has nothing to do with drugs, Dad!"
(Unless you consider great strategy a drug, in which
case I am a dealer, yea!)

It wasn't a mistake when John Roberts opened up his car wash company next door to Dave Martin's Quiky Lube shop. John realized that there was potential working with Dave to grow both of their businesses. In a business sense, they were not competitors, but they both provided one piece of the pie for a customer who was in the market to take care of his car.

By discounting services between them, John and Dave together could make offers that single oil change places and single car washes couldn't make. So the dollars they lost on the discount, they made up for on volume. More people would visit their location to either take advantage of the discount or to just "get it all done in one place."

Are there parallel companies that you could team up with to create natural synergy for the customer? Start viewing your business not as a unique function but as just one piece of the pie in your customer's day. For your average customer using your product or visiting your location, what are other pieces of that pie that you could create a joint venture with to make a win-win-win?

It doesn't always have to be an obvious choice to partner. Sometimes unrelated industries can team up to have some incredible results, as you will see in the following case studies.

Coin Marketing

Starbucks has become the biggest café chain in America. They've managed to get consumers to demand $4 café lattes instead of $1 regular coffee! They've done so in record time.

Last year, Starbucks entered into a very smart partnership with Coinstar. Coinstar is a company that has more than 11,000 little coin counting machines all over America. People put in their loose change and in return get crisp dollar notes and the lowest amount of coins back. For their service, Coinstar charges 8.9 cents on every dollar. But with their joint venture with Starbucks, people won't have to pay 8.9 cents on every dollar as coin counting fees. They can convert 100% of their coins into coupons. Starbucks will pay their fees for them and in return, instead of receiving money in hand, they'll receive Starbucks coupons redeemable at any Starbucks cafés.

People have an advantage as they don't have to pay a coin counting fee. Coinstar benefits as more people will start using them and Starbucks benefits as they get people to come and spend their loose change in their cafes – all for a few cents per person!

Win-win-win!

Action Summary:

- ■ Can you get into a joint venture with your local coin counting machines? Or can you install your own coin counting machines?
- ■ It's a small investment, and the returns could be very good. People could come and convert their loose change into coupons redeemable at your stores.
- ■ How else can you get people to spend their spare change with you?
- ■ Can you enter into a joint venture with nearby stores and restaurants where they can give an option to the consumers to accept either $10 in cash for change or $11 in coupons redeemable at your store? It could work where the store, instead of paying $10 to the consumer, would pay $9 to you on every $11

coupon they distribute. They would save $1 and you would win a new consumer who spends $11 and more, all at a low expense of $2 per person.

Pizza Fliers

One man bought a printing shop in Los Angeles. The printing shop was already doing well and the man could have simply sat back and earned a decent income. But he was entrepreneurial in nature and wanted to increase and expand his business. So he made a list of all his clients. He then made a list of people who reached these clients often and who would also need printing services.

On the top of his list was a pizza place. He contacted the pizza place and asked the owner if he would like to get his pizza boxes printed for free in exchange for inserting fliers that promoted the printing shop. The owner readily agreed and thus started a very profitable barter agreement.

Not much happened during the first few days. But then more orders started coming in from people who lived close to the pizza place. The printing shop's business increased by 200% in a few days! The owner improved the fliers a bit and saw a 300% increase in his business. He got so busy that he was now faced with a new problem: delivering his services on time! He soon had to start a late shift in his small printing shop to keep up with new demand!

Action Summary:

- Make a list of your clients. Then make a list of other people who reach your clients too and enter into joint venture agreements with them.

- Some ideas for joint ventures: you could get them to sell your products, and in return, you could sell their products in your store. You both could place each other's business cards prominently in your stores. You both could share the costs of advertising. You both could merge your shipping services and decrease cost.

- Contact your local pizza place owners and ask them if they would insert your fliers into pizza boxes if you chipped in and paid 10, 20, or 30% of printing costs.

Cool Insurance

Richard Branson has always made hard jobs look fun and cool. Tell him something is impossible, and he'll not only do it, but do it with panache. When people told him that the US insurance market is a tough cookie to crack because of stiff competition, Richard got onto it with a lot of passion and made an ambitious plan to make insurance cool!

A few of his marketing ideas that might end up revolutionizing the insurance industry were leaked to the media (it might have been a marketing gimmick and he might have leaked them himself too). Here are some noteworthy ideas from his plan:

1. *Testing the market: He will roll out Virgin Life Care in Tampa, Florida and San Antonio, Texas, then learn from the test and roll out nationally.*

2. *Copying marketing idea from another industry: Virgin Life will employ a "frequent flier"- like reward program, inspired by the airline industry.*

Virgin will reward points to people who go to the gym. These points can then be redeemed to lower the premiums and to trade in for DVDs and travel services (both offered by Virgin themselves!). The cool thing is how they will go on to reward people with points. Virgin Life will enter into joint ventures with gyms and install "health zones" where members can go to collect points after their workouts. Thus they will receive free publicity from all the gyms themselves!

Action Summary:

- Test out ideas on a smaller scale before spending a lot of money on a big launch. Pre-sell your products to find out how the market will respond.

- Only sell your products in a smaller market to find and get rid of all your kinks in production.

- Observe and learn how firms in other very different industries market themselves and then copy these ideas for your own business.

- Use rewards to build loyalty. Earmark a part of your marketing budget and use it to reward your current clients.

- Be the first in your industry to employ a "frequent flier" type program. Give rewards to people if they do the things you want them to do.

- Enter into joint ventures with other complementary businesses where they can promote you. The simplest way to do this is get a business to showcase your brochures or coupons in their stores.

Barter Tactics

Stephen along with two of his friends started a software programming and Web designing company in 2001. They started off with a few good projects. But earning new business was tough right after the dot-com bust. Their cash flow was decreasing.

One day, due to lack of work and out of boredom, Stephen starts surfing the web and he lands on a web site for a nearby radio station. That web site is a wreck. The radio station doesn't want to spend money on web development and so has assigned one of their clerks to update the web site. The clerk does what he can with the knowledge he has – but the result is an amateurish-looking web site.

Stephen gets an idea when he sees the badly-designed web site. He tries calling the manager of the radio station but gets nowhere. So he then quickly writes his offer down on paper. He gives that offer a curious headline: "How would you like a new and improved web site that will delight your listeners at absolutely no cost to your radio station?"

Stephen then sent the offer letter to the manager of the radio station. Within a week, he is sitting in the office of the manager where he discusses his offer:

1. Stephen would design a web site for the radio station.
2. He would also create a content management system which
3. would make updating the site as easy as sending email.
4. In return, the radio station would pay Stephen no money.
5. Instead, they would provide him with $12,000 worth of
6. radio spots for free ($1,000 a month for an entire year).
7. And during the next 6 months, every time the new radio station's web site URL was announced on air, they would also mention Stephen's company.

Over the next 12 months, Stephen's 3-man company expands! It's estimated that he receives 120 new clients directly because of the barter deal with the radio stations!

Action Summary:

- Radio, TV and other media stations are very influential as they can reach thousands of people.
- Can you barter your products or services with them in return for free advertising?
- If you can't barter directly with these media stations, how about a 3-way barter? For example: you could barter with a restaurant with your services and receive $6000 worth of free meals. You could then approach the media stations and offer them $6000 worth of free meals in return for $5000 worth of advertisements.

Golf Course Promotion

The Claw is the golf course originally built for students at the University of South Florida (USF). Until some time back, they hadn't done a lot to attract other people besides students to their golf courses.

All they did to promote the golf courses is run a few ads in magazines and send special offers to the University alumni. Because of the huge student population, they didn't do too badly. But there was a lot of room for improvement. Then Jim Fortson, the head of the Claw at USF, heard about "joint ventures." He put up a few joint ventures that have worked extremely well to increase the number of people who've bought rounds of golf at the Claw. Here are some of the things he did:

1. *He partnered with travel and tourism groups and companies that have developed special golf packages for their clients.*
2. *He went and did the same thing with local hotels. Many of*

them came out with special "stay and play" packages.

3. *He went and joint ventured with special affinity groups and churches to hold their golf tournaments at the Claw.*

4. *He piggybacked on another hot sport – basketball.*

At the end of 2005, he came up with "Birdies and Buckets" plan where people would receive 4 free tickets to the next USF men's basketball game if they bought 4 rounds of golf. These joint ventures have helped the Claw to get a steady stream of new golfers every month!

Action Summary:

- Joint venturing with other businesses that deal with the same kind of clients as yours is a super idea to gain new clients very cheaply. Three steps to joint venturing:

    1. *Figure out who your clients are.*

    2. *Figure out where your clients go and who they do business with.*

    3. *Approach these businesses with a joint venture proposal showing them how they'll benefit through the venture.*

- Piggybacking on current hot trends is another great idea to sell your products. Giving away free tickets to a current sport always works in selling products quickly.

- Make a deal to get tickets at a discount if you buy them in bulk and then give them away to people who buy more than a certain amount of products from you.

- You could piggyback on other products too. For example: you could give away tickets to the latest movie. This would be much cheaper than giving away tickets to a sport.

Product Tours Marketing

A makeup artist wanted to find more clients but didn't have money to promote her business. So marketer Wendy McClelland came up with a great joint venture idea for her. Wendy told the makeup artist to go approach the local bridal stores, and ask them if she could have a free bridal make up demonstration in their shops on a Saturday. The shops could promote their free bridal makeup demonstration and attract more clients. The makeup artist would then go to the bridal shop on Saturday and ask shoppers to enter a drawing for a free makeover by submitting their names and addresses. She would select one winner from all the entries and do a live makeover for her.

One lucky woman won a free makeover while other women received a few tips on applying makeup. While others watched, the makeup artist would also pass on her brochures to everyone in the crowd.

The best part was, because of the free drawing she created a mailing list of women who were about to get married. She followed up with these women and won more business. She started receiving many clients because of the joint venture with the bridal shop. The idea worked so well that she started holding the bridal makeup demonstration every Saturday!

Action Summary:

- ■ Creating such joint ventures is a win-win situation.
- ■ Here are the steps to take:
    1. *Figure out who your best clients are.*
    2. *Figure out where they hang out.*
    3. *Go to that place and demonstrate your product or service.*

■ Till now, only authors and entertainers have figured out the power of live demonstrations and tours to sell their products. But there is no reason why you can't use the tactic too. Take your products on a tour. Demonstrate them in various shops and marts.

Billboard Radio

Jack owns an antique shop. To promote his antique shop, he buys billboard signs on the expressway – near the exits. The billboard signs are very typical. They have Jack's antique shop logo with a few furniture pictures and very few words. The only words used on the billboard tell people which exit to take to reach the shop. Jack runs these billboard signs month after month.

One day, he listens to a new radio station. The format for that radio station is oldies. Jack immediately calls the radio station and makes an appointment to meet the manager. He then meets the manager and makes him a proposition. Jack would promote the radio station for free on all his billboards if the radio station promotes Jack's shop in return. The manager finds value in the idea. They were going to buy billboard signs to promote the new radio station as it is. This barter deal would help them save some money. They could run Jack's ads when they have some ad spots to fill in. Jack did have to pay a price to repaint part of his billboard signs. The radio advertising he received in return more than made up for this added expense.

Their joint venture worked so well that they were thinking of coming up with a show about antiques on the radio!

Action Summary:

- Contact the local radio station or newspaper and ask them if they would advertise your company for free in return for being promoted by you.

- You could promote them by placing signs in your stores or by placing signs with your current advertising.

- If you already advertise on billboards, you could do what Jack did. If you run direct mail campaigns, you could add a brochure of theirs with the mailing. The idea is to exchange advertising: receive free advertising in return for promoting the advertisers.

The Personal Experience Factor
"And they're bringing their friends"

The world of marketing is changing rapidly. Interconnectivity is becoming a dangerously powerful beast. A business has to provide all that they promise in their advertising. The personal experience factor must be positive. When customers go to a business, they better experience everything promised and more. Because if the advertising is saying that there is superior customer service, but the customers are telling a different story, the business loses.

Beware of the power of failing to meet the mark that advertising sets. With cell phones, Internet, blogs and email having emerged, a powerful new medium has been born. I call it "THEY". You will see the power of "THEY" grow as the technology grows.

Let me describe this new medium. "THEY" is the people who say stuff. The rumors that are spread are a product of "THEY." Have you ever heard about a movie that really stunk? "THEY" say that you get cheated at XYZ Mechanics shop. "THEY say vitamin C is good for the common cold." "THEY say the Cowboys have a great chance of going all the way this year." "THEY say the *Ocho Caliente* can remove all your facial hair with one stroke, sometimes your jaw." The voice of the consumer has always been there, but with new technologies, it is becoming ever louder.

People are dying to have an opinion and to look knowledgeable about things they don't care to do the research to find out about. When it comes to your product or your client, what do people think they know? I hope that the marketing strategy is being supported at all levels of the business. "THEY" can work for you and be some of the best marketing there is, or "THEY" can be a dangerous foe if the customer is failed.

Breaking the Banking Rules

One of the easiest ways to make money is by investing other peoples' money. Borrow money by promising to give a low interest rate to people. Then use that money to make more money.

When people first understood this simple concept, they opened the first banks. Today, banking is one of the most fiercely competitive industries. You can't attract people to lend you money if your deposit rates are lower than your competition and if you can't get people to lend you money, you won't have money to invest and make a fortune for yourself.

Thus in order to grow in the banking industry, a bank has got to give a better interest rate than other banks. The only other way to grow in the banking industry is to merge with or buy another company outright!

One bank based in Missouri broke all the banking rules and shook the industry with their success. Commerce Bank didn't offer the lowest interest rates in their market. They've never made an acquisition either and yet, they were one of the fastest-growing banks in the U.S.

How did Commerce Bank manage to break all the banking secrets to success and yet emerge as one of the most successful banks?

They tried thinking about people before profits. Commerce Bank's mission statement is threefold: "Be Accessible, Offer Solutions, Build Relationships."

Commerce Bank opens their branches seven days a week while the competition is open only five and a half days. They think about their customers' convenience. They spend more money on training staff and they make sure that every employee is friendly and jolly. Commerce Bank does a lot of little things that no other bank does to wow the customers. They like providing fresh coffee to everyone. They give away free newspapers and have installed coin changing machines.

By simply offering better services and going that extra mile, Commerce Bank has grown by leaps and bounds even though they offer a worse interest rate than other bigger banks. Commerce Bank provides an experience to people that no other bank does and in the process, it has made people extremely loyal to them.

Action Summary:

- You can gain a bigger market share even if you don't have the best price in the market by providing better services.
- Do a bit extra and you will wow your clients. Provide better services and people will become loyal.
- Remember: you aren't only selling a product, but an experience too.

The Ritz-Carlton Secret Service

Ritz-Carlton is one of the most successful chains of luxury hotels in the world. They have over 50 hotels all over the world – from Tokyo to Paris to Singapore to New York. One of the main reasons they are at the top of their industry is because of their employment strategy. Bruce Seigel, a director at one of the Ritz-Carlton hotels, says that they hire great people even for the lowest paid positions with extreme care. "We don't hire, we select," Seigel says. "I can teach anyone to make soup, cut lemons, or serve a drink, but I can't teach people to be warm, genuine, friendly and kind. So we identify those talents in the individuals we hire because our brand stands for that kind of care and comfort."

The Ritz-Carlton has made a name for pleasing people. Not

only other competing hotels observe them closely to learn from them; other Fortune 500 companies also keep a close eye on what they are up to. They are one of the best in satisfying customers. Everyone could learn a few tricks from them.

But Ritz-Carlton didn't always enjoy such high customer satisfaction ratings. In fact, in some focus group surveys, they found out that returning guests didn't feel welcomed at all. After searching for a few solutions to solve this problem, they found a great one. To improve their satisfaction levels, and to make the returning guests feel welcome, Ritz-Carlton decided to use the sweetest sound people could ever hear:

Their own names!

Every employee that comes into contact with guests is given radio earpieces. From doorman to bellhop, everyone has to wear an earpiece. This does make them look like Secret Service agents. But it has tremendously improved the customer satisfaction levels. Information about the guests is continuously transmitted through the earpieces. Guests feel like each and every employee of the hotel recognizes them by their names. Not only that, employees can also make comments to the guests about special occasions such as honeymoons and make them feel special. As a result of their secret service-like attire, Ritz Carlton receives 90% guest satisfaction scores; one of the highest for any business. By personalizing greetings for each guest, they made them feel welcomed and special!

Action Summary:

■ The sweetest word a person hears is her own name. Use it to your benefit. Personalize your greetings. Personalize your letters, emails, and postcards with people's names.

■ Make and maintain a database that has your customer names
and information about their likes and dislikes on file.

Hotel at Home

Starwood hotels bought Westin hotels and resorts, a chain of
120 hotels in 24 countries, in 1997 in a move to expand their hotel
empire. Westin hotels had been innovative from their beginning,
being the first hotel chain to implement credit card reservation and
checkout systems way back in 1983 and even in 1997, Westin had a
good reputation. Their customer satisfaction ratings were high. Starwood hotels could have just let Westin be as it was and they would
have made a good profit on their investment. But the then chairman
of Starwood hotels had other ideas.

He didn't want to just satisfy the people who stayed in one of
the Westin rooms. He wanted to delight them. He wanted to give
them the best experience they have ever had staying in a hotel. So
he invested in the basics: the furniture and accessories in the rooms.
He started with the beds. Starwood brought in 50 different types of
luxurious beds for the executive staff, who were to decide which one
of those 50 beds would go in all of the hotel rooms. In the end, they
went with one of the most expensive beds out there in the market.
The beds were fit for a king. Going against hotel industry common
sense, they bought all-white bed sets – complete with cushy white
pillows and pillowcases. They appropriately named the beds "heavenly beds." The beds worked their magic. They delighted the guests
who stayed in the rooms. The beds were so good that people started
talking about it – creating a buzz. Westin hotels soon invested in
"heavenly baths" and "heavenly cribs" too.

These investments in accessories paid up very well as more guests started coming back to Westin. But these investments had a very profitable side effect too. It created a whole new stream of income for Westin hotels. People loved the "heavenly bed" and "heavenly bath" accessories so much that they started asking Westin managers where they could buy them for their own homes. In the first week of introducing the bed, 32 people inquired about where they could buy the beds!

Soon, Westin had to come out with a catalog, phone ordering systems, and an ecommerce web site to sell the accessories. Over a 6 year period, Westin has sold more than 6,000 beds and 30,000 pillows! That is a lot of money when an entire bed set costs $3,115! Westin sold $8.5 million worth of accessories in one year alone, and frankly, they didn't have to do a lot to sell the accessories!

Action Summary:

- ■ Invest in the basics of your product. What will make your products better?
- ■ Delight people. Think about what you can do that will make your clients go "oooh!"
- ■ Find hidden assets that you could sell to generate a new stream of cash flow.
- ■ Is there a part of your product that people would love to buy (e.g., accessories)? Or can you make a new product for your company that people would buy (e.g., Yankees sell caps)?

King of the Beer Men

The food service giant took on a challenge: to find out who the king of the beer men is, the one who sells more beer than anyone in American baseball stadiums. They searched all the stadiums and came up with one guy: Danny!

They then looked at what Danny does that no one else does to sell more beer than any other beer man in America and learned a few cool tricks. While other beer men ask permission to serve 8, 10, 12 or even 15 aisles, Danny asks for only 4 aisles. He focuses on a narrower audience and because of that, he starts remembering names of many of the regulars and season ticket holders and often calls them by their names. Because he just handles 4 aisles, he can also complete his rounds in 20 minutes flat. He thus makes more rounds than any other beer man and sells a lot of beers to the same people and the last thing Danny does is – spends more time with customers than is required.

While other vendors leave during the middle of the 8th inning, Danny goes back to the stands to thank his customers and shake hands with everyone – seat by seat, aisle by aisle. Danny has built a strong loyalty bond. Even if a vendor sneakily comes into Danny's section to sell beers, no one buys from him. Some of Danny's customers' reactions:

- ■ "I don't even like Budweiser, but I buy only from Danny" – Barbara S.
- ■ "I happen to be sitting elsewhere tonight. But I came here to buy from Danny" – Kip P.

As a result of his personal service, Danny sells more beer serving 4 aisles than others sell serving 8 or even 12 aisles.

Action Summary:

- ■ Don't cast a wide net. Instead focus on a smaller target audience. Don't stretch yourself. Instead choose the biggest audience you

can serve well and then stick with it. Danny could have easily
gotten permission to serve 8 aisles, but he stuck to 4.

- It's easier to make a repeat sale to an existing client than to find
a new client. Focus on making repeat sales.
- Don't sell. Serve.
- Personalize your selling and treat people. Instead of simply
ringing transactions, focus on building relations and you'll end
up selling more.
- Thank your clients after the transaction.

Bookstore Buzz

It's 1996 and Jeffrey has an idea. The whole "Internet" thingy
is gaining momentum and Jeffrey thinks that he can start a web site
that sells all the books ever published. The idea is sound. He won't
have any real estate costs. His inventory costs will be extremely low
and he could pass on these savings to shoppers by pricing his books
lower than the usual brick-and-mortar book stores. Jeffrey Bozos
quickly buys a domain and starts amazon.com. Amazon.com starts
with great fanfare and it receives free publicity from the media.
But amazon.com isn't making any profit. Even though their books
cost less than other bookstores, the amount people have to pay for
shipping takes away all the cost benefits (this is before amazon.com
started its free shipping on orders over $25 offer).

People buy from amazon.com for the new experience, but very
few people are loyal to amazon.com. Repeat purchases are very
low. So Jeffrey sits down and thinks of a few ideas. He could spend
money advertising amazon.com and generate new sales. But instead,
he diverts a part of his advertising budget for another cause: that of
delighting prospects. In every delivery box that is shipped, amazon.

com sends coffee mugs and classy bookmarks for free. Customers love the freebies and start talking about it. More importantly, amazon.com builds a base of intensely-loyal clients who shop with them repeatedly.

Action Summary:

- Before spending money on advertising to generate new clients, spend money on delighting your current clients. It's way cheaper to persuade current clients to buy again than it is to persuade people to become clients.
- It doesn't take much to delight people. All you have to do is give them more than you promised. Over-deliver.
- Don't tell them everything you will do for them.
- Surprises delight people.
- Nothing will help you generate more buzz than small unexpected bonuses.
- Even a low-cost item like bookmarks can delight people and create loyalty. You don't have to spend a lot of money to over-deliver.

Real Estate Success

Percy is a real estate agent. He started in a small way but reinvested the bulk of his profits into advertising and promotions to grow his business. He did a lot of newspaper and radio advertising to generate new business. But one day, he sat down to calculate how well his ads were working.

He started asking new clients how they heard of him. Some people were vague and couldn't remember whether they heard about Percy on the radio or read about him in the newspapers. No one was extremely specific as to name the radio station and the time when he heard one of Percy's ads. But it gave Percy a general idea of how people heard about him and which media worked best. But one thing that Percy found surprised him. As many as 35-40% people heard about him through other past clients. Percy thought that if as many as 40% people came to him for free, how could he improve this referral rate even further? He came up with a simple but a novel idea.

He started sending a booklet to his clients a week after they had purchased their house. The booklet was 4 pages long and had the headline: "<Client Name's> Home Sweet Home". Below it was a glossy color picture of their new house. The 2nd page inside the booklet had another headline that simply read "The Search." The whole 2nd page and half of the 3rd page listed smaller pictures of various other houses they visited and the date and time they visited each of them. Below each picture was a caption that gave a reason as to why that house wasn't selected by his clients. The other half of the 3rd page had another headline: "The Choice" and stated reasons as to why the house was chosen. The 4th page had a headline that read "Negotiations" and listed the offers and counter offers. It was followed by "Financing" which listed the lending institution, the interest rate and other mortgage details. That was followed by Percy's photo and his contact information.

Percy didn't pinch pennies while creating this booklet. He made the booklet look so good that his clients could place it proudly on the coffee table. Soon after Percy started printing and sending booklets, he found that he would receive an average of 2-3 referrals from each and every one of his clients. He has reduced his advertising budget drastically because these booklets, which cost $3.50 to print and mail, have increased his referral business by leaps and bounds!

Action Summary:

- An after-sale memento is a great idea. It delights your clients. Plus it gives them something that they can show to their friends and be proud of.
- If you sell low-priced products and can't afford a $3.50 color booklet for each client, simply send a postcard that could be placed on the refrigerator.
- Send a good-looking frameable certificate to them.

100% Closing Strategy

Mr. Jones is a jeweler in Idaho. He runs a series of marketing steps to sell jewelry to his prospects 100% of the time. Here is his system:

1. *He talks to his prospect either in person or by phone.*
2. *He then sends three unset polished diamonds to the prospects so that they can make a choice as to which diamond to use.*
3. *He then sends a few rough designs by email.*
4. *Next he sends them a FedEx package. The package has one video and a pack of microwave popcorn with a note asking them to enjoy the popcorn while viewing the video.*
5. *The video starts with the name of the prospect in the opening title. It then shows the diamonds and gems in three different settings from all the angles so that it's easier for the prospect to make her decision.*

This system has never let Mr. Jones down and whenever he makes use of this elaborate system and sends the video to a prospect, he has managed to make a sale 100% of the time!

Action Summary:

- You might not be selling as expensive a product as jewelry and might not have huge profit margins. But with today's software and technology, it's very easy for you to personalize your sales messages with the receivers' names on it very cheaply.
- Personalization of messages improves sales chances every time.
- First find out what people want. Then give them a limited choice of solutions.
- Don't give them 20 choices so that they get overwhelmed and confused.
- Don't just give one solution which would give them no say at all in the decision-making process. Show them how each solution would work.

Accounting Certificate

Hugh runs his own one-man accounting firm. He decided to start making monthly "health" reports for his clients. Every month, he will give a 4-page report to his clients showing a summary of profit-and-loss statements, increase in sales and profits since last month, any upcoming big payments and a few more things.

Every report has a small blurb about Hugh and his services on it. Hugh created such a health report for 2 of his clients. One of his clients already referred his services to his associates. Now that Hugh has a template for the health report made, it shouldn't take him more than 20 minutes per client per month to plug in the numbers and print out the report. Twenty minutes is worth the effort to satisfy clients and make them aware that Hugh is the best accountant in town.

Action Summary:

- A "memento" or a booklet is a great item to give to your clients. It's a small thing that will show them you worked harder than was required and it will delight them.

- My suggestion to Hugh: accounting information is private. Not many business owners will show the health report to their associates. But yet, his clients have already referred Hugh's services to their friends. One thing Hugh can do to facilitate his clients referring him is – give away 2-3 business cards with every health report.

- Hugh could also attach a note specifically asking his clients to give away his business cards to their associates.

- You could do the same: create 4-page special reports for your clients, and attach a few of your business cards to it.

Sell an Experience
Yes! I want Jazz Hands!

Perception is reality! This statement rings true as it runs throughout the business of marketing. People make their decisions on "their" reality. As a company, it is important that you have a good perception out there, creating all of these realities. People want an experience. Can you take your product, or the way you do business and make it into something more than what it is? Knock the personal experience factor through the roof. People pay big bucks to have the "experience of a lifetime"; use this to your advantage to grow a simple shopping trip into an amazing time. Remember, the wedding is for the couple, the reception is for everyone else. Ever notice all the really great stories come from the reception? (And yes, I am aware that another factor is that the reception is where the alcohol is too. But that makes it an experience, right?)

Rock & Roll Theatres

With the advent of new technology, fewer people are going to movie theatres. The problems are many. People are buying big screen televisions for their home and no longer go to cinemas. Because of the Internet and high-speed broadband connections, it's easy to share movies with others and watch them at home within a day of their release. No wonder that the admissions to movie theatres fell by 4% in the year 2003 according to the Motion Picture Association of America.

To counter the loss of revenue and profits, many movie theatres are coming up with ingenious ideas. Some are installing love seats to make it even more fun for couples to come see a movie. Others are selling beer in multiplexes to attract a whole new audience and one chain of theatres named "Alamo Drafthouse" started offering a complete package of "dinner and movie."

Regal Cinemas, which owns and operates 5,300 screens all over America, however, has the best approach. They started broadcasting live concerts and shows in the movie theatres. They spent some money and overhauled their theatres. They installed digital sound systems and stadium-style seating in their theatres. Now people could either go to Las Vegas or LA to watch a live concert or they could go to their own town and watch the second best thing: live concerts on the big screen. The atmosphere here would be electric too. The audience would erupt after the end of songs and dance along with the tunes.

People are willing to pay as much as $15 instead of the $9 they pay for a movie ticket because the concert is live and the theatres are always packed on all the nights when there are live concerts. All this happened because someone in Regal Cinemas decided that they were in "the business of entertaining, not just screening movies."

Action Summary:

- Most companies wait for bad times before they start implementing new tactics. You don't wait for bad times. Be prepared. Brainstorm on how you can use the resources you currently have to provide more value.
- Sell an experience. Cinemas increased their ticket sales when they offered "love seats." How can you do something special for a target audience?
- Don't be affected by marketing myopia.
- The train industry declined because they thought they were

in the "business of tracks and trains" instead of the "business of transportation." They kept on improving the trains without realizing that people wanted better transportation, not better trains.

■ Think how you can help your audience instead of how you can improve your bottom line. It will happen when the audience is pleased.

Check and Mate

John invested in a small business. He purchased a "hobby and game" store that had been run profitably for the past 30 years. The old owner wanted to retire and thus John was able to receive a great deal on the shop. Soon after he bought the store, John found out that all was not right. The store had been neglected for a long time. The old owner had not bought any new merchandise in the last 10 months. Due to the decline in new kinds of games at the store, the longtime loyal buyers had stopped visiting. In addition to that, the months-long liquidation sale had attracted the wrong type of people to the store – the deal seekers who only wanted discounts and cheap products!

John knew he had to change something fast to attract the right kind of people again. To spread the word fast, he started hosting games and tournaments. He started hosting different kinds of tournaments to attract a different but more lucrative kind of clients. One week, he would host chess and other similar strategy game tournaments that appeal to the older clientele. The next week, he would host "HeroClix" and "Magic the Gathering" which were popular among the teenagers. Word about his store spread like wildfire within no time.

The tournaments attracted tons of people to the store. It allowed the customers to interact with the store and check out the employees and the store merchandise. That's not all - the game tournaments had one more advantage: they allowed people to connect with each other and become loyal to the store. Tournaments are great loyalty builders!

Action Summary:

- A contest or tournament is a great way to attract people and increase profits.
- The competition and the interaction between people that tournaments allow build customer loyalty.
- How can you involve your store location or your merchandise in a tournament or contest?

King of All Movie Theatres

Movie theatres are having a rough time. Piracy of movies affects them badly. So do the improvements in technology. Many people have flat screen TVs and surround sound systems in their homes now and thus they don't go to watch movies in theatres as often as they used to. As a result, movie theatres witnessed a 4% decline in their ticket sales in one year! But all this doesn't seem to affect one movie theatre. In fact, instead of performing badly like many other theatres are doing, they actually did quite well.

Muvico Theatre in Maryland, which has 24 screens, is the most successful movie theatre in America selling more tickets than any other theatre for 2 straight years! How do they perform so well in an industry hit by many grave problems? Muvico doesn't sell tickets to movies.

They sell tickets to a completely novel experience. They've spent a lot of money on the interior decorations of the theatre. The Muvico looks like an ancient Egyptian tomb. They have erected a statue of Anubis - the Egyptian god of the dead! The walls have detailed hieroglyphics. The ambience is fantastic and surreal. If they wanted to, they could sell tickets to people just to take a tour of the theatre! Muvico further raises the bar by providing great customer service. Like other movie theatres, Muvico makes most of its money selling popcorn at the concession stands. But unlike other movie theatres, there are no long lines of people waiting their turn and missing the beginning of their movies.

On busy nights, Muvico uses as many as 23 cash registers and employs as many as 45 people to staff the concession stands. They keep the lines short and the movie watchers happy and on top of that, Muvico does one more thing that makes them the king of all movie theatres. They realize that they could have the best ambience and provide the best experience, but no one would buy tickets if they didn't show good quality movies. So Muvico employs more screens to show hit movies. It's not uncommon at Muvico to see 2-3 movies being shown on as many as 15-18 screens at the same time. Muvico tries to service the masses instead of the classes and thus they only show premier Hollywood movies to fill up the seats.

At a time when there are dozens of other choices people have instead of seeing movies, Muvico attracts the masses by showing only the best movies, providing the best customer service, and selling a novel experience!

Action Summary:

- ■ Sell an experience to your clients. Invest in your ambience. Make your place of business look attractive and you'll see a lot more people come to you than go to your competition.

■ Give more shelf space to products that have a higher demand. Don't try to sell everything. You'll make more money selling only a few highly-demanded products.

■ The movie theatres have learned that they can make more profits at the concession stands than by actually showing movies.

■ Look out for products that complement your current line of products.

■ What could people buy from you that would allow them to gain even more from your products?

Give to Get

You scratch my back, I'll let you scratch it again…
OK, fine, I'll scratch yours

At the end of the day, when the advertising budget is spent, the result that the business owner hopes to achieve is to have more customers come in and the cash register to ring. In the mind of many marketers this means spending the budget on media or print to inform the public of an offer or value. There are times and products that will allow for a technique I call "give to get."

This technique considers the cost of goods to be part of the marketing budget. A company will use their product or service to make an offer to the public that will motivate them to come to the business.

This worked well for a little pizza company called Davey's Pizza. The owners of this pizzeria were in a quandary as to how to grow their business in their small town. One of the local television affiliates came in and produced a commercial featuring their pizza, price and location. They encouraged the owners to extend their advertising budget from the $400 they were comfortable with to just over $700 a month for a three-month deal. The results were less than spectacular and they overextended themselves with the $2100 investment.

When asked, "What would have made that campaign successful?" the owners explained that their pizza was so incredible, that once a customer had it, they were customers for life. They believed that if they could have had 100 new customers, their $2100 investment would have paid for itself over time.

A supreme pizza cost Davey's Pizza $4.00 to make. The owners had been able to scrape up a $300 budget to use. This was a difficult task considering that they were already overextended from the earlier deal. The goal was getting 50 new clients to try their pizza. They were concerned because $2100 didn't yield the 100 they wanted, how could one seventh of the budget pull in 50 new customers?

They kept the first $100 back as the cost of the pizza. They purchased a $50 radio spot during the evening drive and ran this script:

"Good evening. Are you feeling hungry? Davey's Pizza is interested in buying twenty-five of you dinner tonight. One large, multi-topping pizza, cooked fresh. All you have to do is call and then swing in and pick it up. That is assuming you're one of the first twenty-five callers. I know that when you hear a deal like this, you get skeptical. I assure you there is no catch. We are so confident that once you try a hot Davey's Pizza, we will be the place you keep coming back to. We are so confident that we are willing to buy your first one. So, that's the deal. The first 25 callers get one large, multi-topping Davey's Pizza for Carry out. It's 5:25pm right now; you can even make the call on your cell phone and pick it up before you go home. 555-1234"

Realize that the salesperson or ad agency would most likely never come up with or recommend this idea. They usually get paid on the commissions of the dollars that get spent. If the commission rate was 15%, then by going from a $2100 media purchase to a $50 media purchase, the salesperson's commission went from $315 to $8. Most advertising and broadcast companies work in this manner and would be hesitant to give up the revenue.

Davey's Pizza was ecstatic with the results. The phones blew up. The first 25 pizzas were gone in no time. Many of the recipients of the free pizza added extra pizzas to the order. They had a special rate set up for those callers who missed the first 25 but still wanted to order. The pizza orders were rolling in. There were way more than 25 new customers that night, as well as $150 left in the advertising budget to do this again on another night, for an additional 25. Davey's Pizza, with the total $300 budget, outperformed the 'one hundred new customers' goal that was not reached by the $2100 budget campaign.

There are other ways to do this, even if you are not in the food industry. A dentist can give away free toothbrushes, or a jeweler can do watch batteries for free. The goal is to get a customer in so that you can get a shot at developing a relationship or showing your products. But what if you are a service industry?

A local insurance agent wanted to write more policies. Her competitors were running ads saying that they can beat your current auto rate by "up to 40%." I asked her if it was true. She said that there might be one person that is getting such a bad deal somewhere that 40% might be doable, but you also had to carry your homeowners with them. Overall they never get close to even 20%.

I asked her to make a deal with a local restaurant and get some $20 gift certificates. Knowing that she was going to be handing out a lot of them and mentioning them in the advertising, the restaurant gave her the certificates at half price. She then advertised:

"Many insurance companies claim to be able to beat 15, 20 even up to 40% below your current auto quote. Of course once you get there, you learn that you have to have multiple policies with them and even then, that 40% goal usually is out of reach. At the J. Ford Insurance Agency, I am shooting straight like I always do. I will try to beat your current insurance rate by 30%, apples to apples. If I am unable to meet the 30% mark, I will send you to Ghepetto's Fine Dining with a $20 gift certificate. That is my thank you for giving me the opportunity to earn your business. No catch. Just bring your current insurance policy in, and if I can't beat it by 30%, you get a trip to Ghepetto's, the home of the freshest Italian food in town. I want to earn your business."

The truth is that she is planning on sending most of the people who come in to dinner. Thirty percent is a very difficult number to beat, but that will bring in a large number of people looking for a great discount or a free dinner. What if the best she can do is beat their current rate by 7%? I bet they would like to save that 7% while they are there, oh and by the way, here is your dinner on us. The dinners didn't cost the agent much and came out of her advertising budget anyway. It's a win/win/win for everyone. The agent gets higher traffic coming in. The restaurant gets people coming to dinner with a coupon, an advertising expense they would spend anyway. Last is the consumer, who gets a great deal on insurance and a dinner at a restaurant that they will probably frequent again.

There is a catch, though: you must be honest. If you can't quite get to the 30% payoff don't be sneaky, because if there is a catch, your plan will backfire. Also, make sure that the company you are partnering with is aware of how many of their items you are planning on giving away. Remember, your marketing dollars are supposed to be used to give you a shot at doing business. Sometimes the results are amazing if you are willing to give a bit to get a shot.

Breaking the Motel Market

One advantage of having a chain of motels is the recognition they receive. People passing through a small town will tend to stay in a motel whose name they have heard before rather than some other local motel, even though the local motel might be better than the chain!

This fact made it tough for a motel in a small town in Southern America as there were 2 other chains competing for new business in the same town. How could the motel effectively promote itself? It would be too expensive to buy airtime on television. What was the motel to do to spread the word among the masses?

How could they reach tourists from other cities who visited their small town and persuade them to stay in their motel? The owner of the motel tried buying ad space in newspapers and magazines. But they weren't successful in bringing in new clients. He tried sponsoring a golf tournament to build some recognition. But that failed to bring in new people too. Finally, one tactic worked. The owner started a low-cost referral program that brought in new business like crazy.

The owner bought many sets of glasses directly from the manufacturer at whole-sale price. Then he sent postcards to everyone in the small town that contained the picture of the set of those beautiful glasses on the front. The postcard asked the people to recommend their friends and business associates who visit the small town to come and stay at their motel. Anyone who showed up at the motel with the postcard would receive a free set of glasses and what's more, the person who refers them to the motel would also be entitled to one set of glasses.

For the price of two glass sets at wholesale value, the motel beat their competition and was flooded by business.

Action Summary:

- Providing incentives to people to refer others works great. A reward gives a reason to people to come and do business with you instead of your competitors.
- The motel changed its target audience from tourists to friends and associates of locals. The right target market can work wonders for your business.

Valentine's Pizza

John owns a very small pizza parlor. But the size of his parlor isn't a deterrent for his business as about 80% of his orders are for home delivery. Like most other pizza parlors, John did very good business on weekends and holidays.

Except one holiday, that is. On Valentine's Day, John would sell the lowest amount of pizzas. It seemed like very few people ate pizzas on February 14th every year. Instead they would go out to a much more expensive restaurant. John decides to tackle this problem and bring in more orders on Valentine's Day. It was a mighty challenge for him and thankfully, John was able to find a solution - a very easy and low-cost solution that brought a flood of orders to his parlor on February 14th! The solution? John started a marketing campaign: Receive one free rose with every pizza ordered on Valentine's Day.

John then sent a simple press release to the local radio and TV station on February 13th - a day before Valentine's Day. He got some coverage on one of the media outlets. His sales hit the roof on what was the slowest day for every other pizza outlet!

Action Summary:

- ■ What low-cost bonus can you give away with your product that will make people go "cool" and "wow" and persuade them to buy from you instead of your competition?
- ■ You could steal this idea outright. Give away a rose or even a box of heart-shaped chocolates for every purchase on February 14th.
- ■ You could also send press releases to the media a few days beforehand and try to receive some free publicity.

The Salon Referral Contest

Lily owns a salon. Her salon is small, and she is the only employee. She manages to work on just about 4-5 people's hair a day – 100 people a month. But her average billing is about $80 per person and thus, she grosses a decent $8,000 a month.

Lily still has a lot of free time when no one visits her salon. Tuesdays and Wednesdays are especially slow. So she hired a marketing consultant. The marketing consultant gave her an ingenious "referral contest" idea. Lily gets a bunch of business cards printed. The front side of the business card is like most other business cards: it gives the name, address and phone number of Lily's salon. But Lily also makes use of the flipside of those business cards.

The flipside of the card reads: "Refer a friend and win one year's worth of free hair care." Below the text, the flipside has two blank spots: one for the name and the other for the telephone number of the referral. Lily starts giving these business cards to all of her current clients and in no time, she starts receiving new clients who have been referred to her - thanks to the new business card "referral contest."

At the end of a few weeks, Lily selects a winner by calculating who referred the most new clients to her. The winner receives a year's worth of free hair care. But Lily places a condition on that too: she gave free hair care during Tuesdays and Wednesdays only – her slowest days. Lily might have had to invest 20-25 hours on the winner throughout the year (about 2 hours a month) and the cost of printing those business cards is $60. But what are the results of the tactic? The referral contest is a big hit. It generates 120 new jobs for Lily over the year. That is a jump of 10% business for Lily's salon. The business card referral contest earns Lily a cool $9,600 for the cost of just $60 and a few hours!

Action Summary:

- Start a referral program. Give incentives to your current clients to promote you and refer their friends to you.
- Run a contest. A contest is a great way to generate a buzz.
- Copy the entire concept and run a "referral contest." Give a big goodie to the winner who refers the highest number of people in a specified period of time.
- Make use of both sides of your business cards. You don't necessarily have to use the flipside as a referral tool.
- You could simply add a client testimonial on that side.

Free Air Safety

Mr. Katz ran an appliance and air conditioning business. He had built his business into a good strong one by making shrewd decisions and providing top service over the years. He was looking to take his business to the next level. He thought he needed to improve his marketing skills. So he went to one of Jay Abraham's marketing seminars.

One of Jay's points made a big impression on Mr. Katz: "If you have confidence in your product, it's very easy to give away free samples and make money in the future by building trust and developing a relationship."

After the seminar was over, he decided to implement a new campaign. He started offering free carbon monoxide detectors and he also offered safety inspection services for free for a limited time. More than 1500 people called and asked for their free carbon monoxide detectors and close to 200 people asked Mr. Katz to come and inspect their residences for safety. It cost about $13,000 to offer the detectors and his services for free to so many people, no small amount by any means. But the returns weren't small by any means either. He did two outstanding things:

1. *He always tried to get these people to upgrade the services they were receiving. He sold his other products and services with every order he received.*

2. *Mr. Katz kept in touch with these people through mail. In a year's time, he tracked that he made $112,000 in sales from the clients generated from his freebie offer program!*

That number jumped to $250,000+ after the end of the second year! A whopping $250,000 in sales from an initial investment of $13,000 is a tremendous achievement!

Action Summary:

■ If you have confidence in your product or service, offer a free sample, or a highly-discounted sample (to avoid making an initial loss and cover costs). Let your free or discounted offer attract interested prospects.

■ Give the best service you can even when the offer is a free one. Build trust and credibility.

■ Then follow up. Contact the people who take advantage of your free offer regularly. Follow up until they buy from you or until they tell you to stop!

■ Try to educate them on why they should upgrade. Make sales on the backend. Track the profits you make from people who took advantage of your free offer. This way, you'll be able to measure what pulls best: your other advertisements or your free offer.

Gas Hike

When gas prices go up car sales go down drastically! One of the biggest car sellers near Detroit – the motor city - was hit by the decrease in sales when the gas prices shot up in just a few months. But unlike other car sellers who blamed the war or the government, they decided to take control of the situation.

They decided to turn the negative news into a positive event. They came up with an offer: they would reduce the car prices by $1 per mile the buyers had traveled to get to the dealership. People started going to them instead of their competitors to buy their cars. People started driving 30 miles to go to this car dealer with the special offer instead of going to a car seller 15 miles away! Even though the total number of cars bought decreased because of rising gas prices, they didn't notice any effect because the ratio of people who bought cars from them went up!

The sweetest thing about the whole campaign is the media got news of it and gave them a lot of free publicity as "positive" gas stories are rare.

Action Summary:

- You could run a similar contest. Give a 10 cent per mile discount.
- Or maybe you could give a flat $10 discount for everyone who has traveled more than 20 miles.
- You can run a contest: the person who travels the longest to buy from you in a given time frame will get all their money back.
- Turn a negative news story into a positive event, and you'll receive a lot of free publicity!

Gift Vouchers Strategy

Steve is an excellent photographer. But he doesn't shoot photos of people. Instead he specializes in shooting photos of pets – mostly dogs. He is a super pet photographer and charges as high as $5000 for a 2-day professional photo shoot session! Until recently, he had to go after people to sell his services. He did everything: bought ads in yellow pages and newspapers, cold called people, sold his services on eBay. But recently, he started using gift vouchers to get people to come to him, instead of him going to them.

He created and custom printed a few gift vouchers that could be redeemed for one hour of a professional photography session. He then approached the pet groomers in his city and gave them these gift vouchers that they could give away to their clients. Quite a few of these groomers' clients took Steve up on his offer and brought their pets for the one-hour free family portrait photo shoot. Steve didn't cut back on these photo shoots even though they were free and he shot the same high-quality pictures he always does for clients that pay him hundreds of dollars. However, he offered only the 8x10 sized family portrait photos for free. If these people wanted bigger pictures and better frames, they would have to buy them. Fortunately Steve is so good at his work that when people see the 8x10 photos, they pay to buy a bigger size of the photo too.

In fact, on average, people who redeem the free vouchers buy as much as $200 worth of extras from Steve! Steve doesn't stop there, though. He then gives these people 3-5 gift vouchers they can give away to their friends too – in effect creating a self-feeding viral marketing strategy.

Today, Steve doesn't have to invest a single dollar in advertising his services and yet people call him everyday to redeem their own free gift vouchers!

Action Summary:

- If you have a high-quality product, give away a free sample. Demonstrate to people how good you actually are by allowing them to test you out without any obligations.
- Create gift vouchers that give away your free sample product to people when they come to your shop.
- Give these free vouchers to other business owners who have the same target audience as you do.
- Also give away the same gift vouchers to people who redeem these gift vouchers and buy your other products too, so they can pass them on to their friends. Create a viral loop for your business.
- You might not want to give away gift vouchers to people who redeem these gift vouchers but don't go on to buy your other products. "Birds of a feather flock together." Freebie seekers will usually give away your gift vouchers to more freebie seekers. People who actually buy from you will give these gift vouchers to others who will also buy from you!

Coffee Hour

Mr. Perez is an investment banker. He uses a simple marketing idea to network with the community and win a prospect's attention for $4 a prospect. What does he do?

He made a convenient arrangement with the local Starbucks. Every Wednesday, from 8:30 a.m. to 9:30 a.m., coffee is on him. Anyone who comes to that Starbucks at that time gets to have free coffee! In return, Starbucks places a poster right next to the payment counter that shows a smiling photo of Mr. Perez, and underneath it is an explanation that says that every Wednesday morning from 8:30

a.m.-9:30 a.m. he buys coffee at that Starbucks for all his customers and anyone else who wants to talk with him about investment banking and Mr. Perez's promising future.

Almost everyone who receives the free coffee goes to thank Mr. Perez who sits in one prominent corner. Usually, there is a bunch of people surrounding him, and conversing with him. Mr. Perez starts a relationship by giving free coffee to prospects. Rarely anyone who drinks the coffee and listens to Mr. Perez talk forgets him. When they need advice in investment banking, guess who they call?

Action Summary:

- Go where your prospects go. Sponsoring one hour at the local coffee shop gives Mr. Perez an opportunity to meet with a lot of rich folks. You could copy his idea too. Maybe offer 50% off if $4 is too expensive.
- Give to get. Offer free coffee, answer people's questions, give out your marketing material and a business card, and you'll soon enough start seeing a lot of those folks come to you for advice.

Stepto's Free Lunch

Mike Stepto's Bar-B-Q Shack in Evansville, Indiana has some great food. You can't drive by his location without the smell of Memphis-style barbecue trying to seduce you off into his parking lot. One of the things Mike wanted to do was to grow his catering business, but he wanted to make sure that diverting his marketing dollars didn't cost him any of his restaurant business. Mike got the idea from another restaurant owner outside of town that would make this possible.

Mike sent out a direct mail piece to local businesses that said:

"You've won a FREE lunch for 10 people in your office!"

When they turned the card over, it said that the first 20 companies that called would get the free lunch and then it supplied the phone number. He even listed a "The Catch" section at the bottom, because in the world of hype we live in, everyone is looking for the catch. It said:

1. *Only the first 20 companies will get a free lunch for 10. I'm mailing this to only a few businesses and I want to be able to personally drop it off and say hello.*
2. *Think of Stepto's BBQ Shack first for your next event – That's it!*

My company took Mike up on his offer and brought lunch in the following Monday for the office staff. Not only did we have a fantastic lunch, I had a few minutes to talk with Mike Stepto, who did exactly as he said and delivered it himself.

Mike won in a few ways that day. One is that our company will consider Stepto's BBQ Shack next time we have an event. They weren't even on the table as an option prior to that day. Our company now knows Mike Stepto on a first-name basis, and that can never hurt.

But it had another effect, one that I know Mike intended. The 10 people who had lunch remembered how great Stepto's was and that they hadn't been there in a while. I guess they could have watched a commercial and had the same thought, but instead they were actually chomping down on one of his brisket sandwiches.

Action Summary:

- Mike Stepto was able to reach 20 businesses in town.
- Those businesses enjoyed a free lunch.
- Those employees were reminded how much they loved the food.
- So for the cost of 50 or so direct mail pieces and food cost, Mike put his BBQ company on the map for events and had 200 people sampling his product.
- Can your company copy this technique to grow your business?

Catering Master

Mark runs a catering business. His prices are higher than most of his competitors. Yet he does more business than most caterers. Here is his marketing strategy:

1. *He runs ads in yellow pages and newspapers. These ads promote a free report that people can receive to read about how they can save money while throwing a party.*

2. *When a person calls in for their free report, Mark takes down their name and address and asks them about their party theme and how many people they are thinking of inviting to their party.*

3. *Mark then sends them the free report within a day and after a few days, he calls them again and asks them if they have any questions for Mark.*

Quite a few caterers do what Mark has done up till now, but what Mark does next makes all the difference.

Mark then goes to the person's place just before lunchtime with a "surprise lunch." This surprise lunch consists of enough food for 4-6 people. With these 4 steps, Mark converts 95% of people who call him for the free report to order catering services from him. Even though his prices per plate are higher, people happily pay them because no other caterer puts in as much effort as Mark does.

Action Summary:

- Mark's strategy in two sentences: "Provide people with free information that helps them make their decisions. Then give them a surprise demonstration." You can copy Mark's strategy for selling higher-end goods and services too.
- Prepare a free report that you can give away to people. The free report can act as a silent salesman promoting your product to people.
- Follow up with people. Contact them after a few days and ask them if they have any questions you can answer.

Money for Time

John is a financial consultant. Whenever he is in need of new business, he buys 1000 leads from a local mailing list broker and mails them a letter. His total cost of mailing 1000 letters is $850 and he usually ends up with 10-12 new appointments from these mailings. Overall, it costs John around $80 to get one new appointment. John converts one in two appointments into a client.

One day, John thinks of an outrageous idea and decides to try it out to see if it'll work better than the previous mailing campaigns or not. He attaches half of a $20 bill to his letter and adds a note to it saying that he promises to give them the other half for 20 minutes of their time. To keep the costs low, he just mails out 100 letters this time. What was the total cost of this mailing? $1135 (including the half-$20 bills). With this mailing, John receives 34 new appointments! John's cost of securing appointments goes down from $80 to $33. When John gets to see the prospect, he gives them the other half of the twenty, thus bringing his cost to $43 per appointment! And this time, because prospects are impressed by John's outrageous idea, 65% of them (22 people) become clients!

Action Summary:

- ■ This is a great idea: send people half a note and promise to give them the other half if they do a particular thing (agree to see you, or fill out a survey or a form, etc.)
- ■ But be cautious. Because this campaign will initially cost a lot more to mail out, only mail such a letter out to a few people. Start by mailing to 50-100 people and seeing if the response is worth it or not.

Free Water Trick

It's 1931, the Depression years. Ted and Dorothy had just bought a drugstore in the middle of nowhere. Ted and Dorothy wanted to live in a small town and they zeroed in on a town called Wall, South Dakota. The population of the town was 326 people.

Ted and Dorothy had bought a drugstore in the new town. They had hopes that the roadway traffic would generate sales. But soon, they found out that people driving by wouldn't stop to go to a store in the middle of nowhere! Ted would stare out of the window for hours at a time and wait (and hope!) that a car would stop and the passenger would come in to the store to buy a thing or two. The cars never did stop! Five years went by; Ted and Dorothy were holding on by a thread. They had decided that if business didn't increase soon, they would have to sell their shop and move.

One day, Dorothy had a bright idea. One hot afternoon, she was trying to take a nap but couldn't sleep. The cars passing by made a lot of noise. She asked herself, what would these car passengers want one hot afternoon driving through the prairies? Why, ice-cold water of course! She convinced Ted to put up a few signs on the highway telling people to come to their store for free ice-cold water!

The people came in droves! Ted and Dorothy were soon filling glasses and giving away free ice water to people. Many of these people would come in for water and end up buying a few items from the store too – items like ice cream and mints! The free ice water offer was an instant success. So much so, that within a year, Ted and Dorothy had to hire 8 girls to help them during the summers.

Today the store is still in the middle of nowhere. But it has grown by leaps and bounds because of drivers stopping by for free ice water! The Wall Drug store has increased their highway advertisements too. You can now see their free ice water signs 500 miles away from their store! Wall Drug store spends close to $300,000 on advertising a year. And all this advertising was not done in vain. Wall Drug store has become a tourist destination and it attracts 20,000 tourists on any single summer day! Their annual sales total more than 11 million dollars! And it all started with the free ice water signs!

Action Summary:

- ■ Sell or give away something that people really want.
- ■ Attract more people to come to your store by giving them a freebie that doesn't cost you much, but is valued a lot.
- ■ Give away something that your competitors don't, and the

customers will form a line outside your store.
- ■ Then advertise your free and unique offer extensively.

Market Domination

Robert started a printing and graphic designing company focused on serving businesses in January of 1995. He knew that there were many other companies offering the same services he did. Because of the computer revolution, more people were jumping on the bandwagon. So Robert made a decision of investing at least one third of his revenue into promoting his company. Thus the company grew faster than most of its competition. But what led to a complete revolution was a brilliant idea Robert had after 5 years of being in business. With *business topology*, he looked at how hotmail.com had grown by adding a tag line "Free email provided by hotmail.com" to all their outgoing email messages. He brainstormed on how he could use that same idea for his purposes. After some thinking he hatched the idea of providing free business cards to people if they didn't mind his adding a small tag line on the back of each of the business cards.

Thus Robert's company, Vistaprint.com, started giving away business cards for free when people paid for shipping and handling. On the back of all the business cards they shipped, they added the tag line "Business Cards are Free at Vistaprint.com" - building a self-fueling viral marketing campaign.

The results? Vistaprint.com is one of the most well-known printing companies and did business of more than 90 million dollars in 2005. Today, the company has more than 5 million current customers who generate 10,000 new orders per day! What's more is that there is no stopping vistaprint.com – they are growing by an insane 100,000 new customers a month because their free business cards are still working overtime for them!

Action Summary:

- Admittedly, it's hard to "force" your clients to spread your word like hotmail.com did or vistaprint.com does. You need to come up with some freebie that you can give away to your prospects that serves 3 purposes:
    1. The freebie is useful.
    2. The freebie is demonstrative and others will be able to see it.
    3. Your company can be advertised prominently on that freebie.
- If the freebie is something that your clients can give away to their friends, that's even better.
- Some ideas: pens, t-shirts and caps, key chains, business cards (you don't have to be a printer to give away free business cards).
- Give away a sample of your product to people and once they are sure about the quality of your work, they will buy more from you.

Restaurant Survey

Gina operates Maggio's Restaurant. Gina knows that for long-term success of the restaurant, she will have to find a cost-effective way to build loyalty between the diners and the restaurant. Gina shells out about $250 and buys a full-page ad in the local newspaper. The ad simply says "Restaurant Survey." The survey asks questions like:

- *How often do you eat out?*

■ *How often do you order delivery?*

To convince people to fill out and mail the survey, Gina offers an incentive of $10 gift certificates to people. Her survey works better than she expects. It brings in more than 2,000 responses! Gina spends time entering the information into a database and she then mails out the gift certificates pronto. The people start coming in droves. Even though Gina just sends 2,000 gift certificates, more than double that number comes to the restaurant over a few weeks time. No diner comes in alone! Gina gets diners to fill in a comments card after the end of their meals. She gets them to give away as much information about themselves as possible and then markets to them on a regular basis. She turns one-time diners into regular patrons by following up with them!

Seeing the success of this "restaurant survey," Gina runs other similar surveys over time. She always tweaks or tests the offer. She finds out that people don't fill out the surveys if they are promised "20% off your check". Nothing works as well as "$10 gift certificates." Not even "free desserts" and "free beverages." So now she sticks with $10 gift certificates.

On restaurantowner.com forum, Gina writes, "When we first started doing this kind of marketing, we thought we were going to be giving away the store, but the truth is, we have increased business by 10% the first year, 20% the second and this past year, 30%!!! And yes, we are making money and our customers are happy and keep coming back for more."

Action Summary:

■ Use "product surveys." They will allow you to gain valuable information about your target market.

- Build a database of people who fill in the surveys.
- Give an incentive in order to get more people to fill in the surveys.
- Then follow up! Send regular updates to these people. Send them news that would help them. Send them new product developments. Send them good wishes.
- Test your offer. Test your message and the medium. Test the words. You never know what works best until you test.

Bookstore Buyback

Bookstores in airports have a big problem. People aren't loyal to them. There are plenty of bookstores in the airport – one at every corner and near every gate and people who buy books from the airport buy them from the most convenient bookstore.

Paradise bookstores, a chain of bookstores located in many airports all across America, decided to take on the challenge. They decided to make people go out of their way and come back to their bookstores to buy their books to read while flying, instead of going to the bookstore nearest their gates. The first thing Paradise bookstores did is to add their bookmark to all the books they sold. The bookmark lists all the stores nationwide that Paradise has. People wouldn't throw away these bookmarks, even though they were ads for Paradise, as they added to their convenience of marking pages.

This didn't do much for Paradise. People would remember them when they saw a Paradise bookstore again. But they wouldn't go out of their way to go shop at a Paradise bookstore.

So Paradise came out with a nifty idea. They started buying back books bought at their stores at half price. They would attach a receipt to the book with tape – making it easy for people to hang on to their receipts and people could come back to any Paradise store within 6 months, show their receipt and return the book they had bought last time for 50% cash back. For example: A person could go into any Paradise store and buy "The World is Flat" paying the retail price of $27.50. She would get a bookmark with all the other Paradise store locations on it and her receipt would be attached to the dust jacket of the book. That person could come back within 6 months to any Paradise store, show the receipt, and return the book for $13.75. The Paradise bookstore would then bump up the price of the book and sell it for around $17-19 as a secondhand book. The person who received $13.75 back would end up buying her other books at Paradise store too.

Action Summary:

- If your products have good demand in the secondhand market, why not start purchasing them from your clients who want to trade up?
- You could buy them back at a lower price if the client saves his receipt, and thus make sure that your clients come to you instead of going to your competition when they make their next purchase.
- You could also attract a whole new target market: people who wouldn't mind paying less money for a secondhand product.
- Make sure you give away your brochures with every product you sell. Brochures are not as useful as bookmarks, and will be thrown away many times. But many people might also save them, and remember you the next time they need to buy something.

Trump Hits Big Time

Donald Trump is known for his flamboyant style, his super-model love interests and his highest-rated reality TV show: The Apprentice. "The Donald" has led a colorful life hitting the highest highs and the lowest lows. Donald Trump is a billionaire. But he wasn't always one. Did you know that he was once the world's poorest person? Yes. He was poorer than the poorest of the third world countries. At one time, he owed 900 million dollars to the world! He had amassed a fortune, lost everything, and came back to claim it all as his own again! This is the story of how he made his first billion.

Even though Donald goes to Wharton school of business as a student, his education hasn't even begun over there. Donald learns most of the real estate tricks of the trade from his father – Fred Trump. Fred Trump earns a small fortune himself, building affordable houses for the masses. Donald likes to think big. He says: "If you're going to be thinking anyway, you might as well think big." Donald sets his goals on building and owning the world's best real estate property. He decides to get involved in real estate on a much larger scale than his father ever dreamt of.

He decides that the best way to build valuable contacts is to join the most exclusive club in New York. He makes it as a member. This is where Donald learns the skills that will allow him to build a billion-dollar fortune twice! Donald learns the psychology of the wealthy by mingling with these rich classes. He makes some valuable contacts because of the club. With contacts came power. Donald now has a base of prospective buyers. The rich are his niche!

Donald now proceeds to secure the world's choicest real estate property in Manhattan to build his first real big venture: The Trump Towers. His idea of building luxury condominiums in one of the most expensive areas in the world is grand. But trouble is right ahead. The New York economy crumbles. By the time Trump Towers is ready for occupancy, nobody wants to buy the high-priced cribs. His competition is killing Donald by further lowering their prices to sell luxurious homes in this bad economy. But Donald doesn't think of cutting prices.

He doesn't join his competition in the frenzy of cheapening his property value. Instead, he uses the psychology of the wealthy to attract them. Instead of cutting prices, Donald offers a complimentary Rolls Royce for free on every condo purchased! Giving a discount on a luxurious property isn't newsworthy. But giving away a Rolls Royce is! Donald Trump's brilliant bonus giveaway tactic earns him free airtime on every major media network!

Donald hits it big time with Trump Towers. People from all over the world now line up to buy condos in Trump Towers.

Action Summary:

- Think big. "If you're going to be thinking anyway, you might as well think big."
- Join clubs and attend parties to build contacts.
- Don't spend time and money in trying to learn sales and marketing. Instead invest time and money in learning human psychology.
- Don't cut prices. Instead raise them and offer a bonus goodie. Some people will choose you over your competition only because of that extra goodie.
- If the goodie is anything as outrageous as an expensive car, you'll also end up receiving tons of free publicity.

İkea Creates a Stampede

People love novelty. That is why, when a new shop opens up in a town, more people visit it in the first week than in the whole next month. Having opened several stores globally, Ikea, the furniture makers, knew this firsthand. That is why they were well prepared for the opening of their first shop in Arizona.

Usually, an Ikea store has 24 cashiers. But anticipating a rush during the first week, they doubled the number of cashiers in their Arizona store. They then opened an additional dirt parking lot at the south side of their store, which could accommodate 500 more cars. They even hired a deejay to entertain the visitors while they waited in the checkout lines. But nothing could have prepared Ikea for the rush.

There were not hundreds, but thousands of people waiting at the doors of the store before it opened at 9 a.m. Even though 500 extra parking spots had been added, many people couldn't find a spot. Can you make a guess as to how long the first person in line to enter the store waited? No, not 3 hours. Not 6 hours. Not even 12 hours.

Scott Cesen, who was the first person to enter the new store, waited for 8 whole days in front of the doors! Eight whole days!

How does Ikea manage to create such a huge rush when they open up a new store? Simple. They offer freebies to the first few people. This time around in Arizona, they announced that they would give away every item in their 2005 catalog to the first person in line. Retail value: Under $5,000 and the next 99 people in line would receive a free chair worth $99. It costs Ikea much less to produce this furniture. In all, Ikea gave away stuff that cost them a couple of thousand dollars to generate a stampede of traffic!

Action Summary:

- Freebies attract a lot of people. Many times, it costs less to give away a few units of products than it would to buy advertising. The result is much better by giving away the products.

- Many of the people who visited the Ikea store and received a free chair also ended up buying more similar chairs to make a set. Many bought a lot more than just chairs!

- You might not be opening a new store, but you could give away freebies to attract traffic for all sorts of reasons. You can strategically give away freebies when you launch a new product. Or when it's your birthday! Or when it's the store anniversary. Just give people a reason and they will rush in droves to collect their freebies.

Nightclub VIP pass

The nightclub business is a trendy business. Through some unknown criteria, the masses decide which club is "happening" on a particular night of the week. Some clubs will be the rage on Mondays but be total duds on Tuesdays. This is the case even if the club plays the same music on both the days.

One such nightclub was known for being the most happening club on Wednesdays. There would be huge lines outside the club on Wednesdays. But Fridays were another story. The nightclub always took a loss on Fridays. The owner of the nightclub wanted to change all that. He started a marketing campaign to pack the nightclubs on Fridays.

On one particular Wednesday, they start giving away a VIP pass. The pass is as big as a credit card and offers free admission to two people before 10 P.M. on a Friday night. Without the VIP card, people would have to pay a $5 cover charge.

The result of the campaign is quick. Some people who came on Wednesday came to the club on Fridays too. Many who couldn't come, gave away the VIP pass to a friend. Within 2 weeks, the nightclub was jam-packed on Fridays too.

By enforcing the 10 P.M. deadline on the VIP card, the nightclub made sure people came to it before they thought of going to any other nightclub and the people who would come in a bit late would already find the nightclub crowded and feel that it's "happening."

Action Summary:

- Give an incentive to your current customers to come and shop with you again.
- You could give away free entry. You could give a discount on repeat purchases. You could give loyalty points that can be redeemed at your own store at a future date.
- Make your current customers bring their friends to your store. The nightclub did this by offering free admission to two people on one VIP card. You could give a bonus to a person if she brings a friend with her.
- A crowd generates a bigger crowd. Make your store seem busy to attract more people.
- Create the illusion of being busy by having inbound calls be placed on hold for a few minutes (even if you are available).
- Make people perceive that you are in demand. You will find that your demand actually increases.

The Gift Certificate Power Offer

Murphey, a jeweler, was in trouble. It was December, and he had to generate $50,000 within a month. On top of that, his sales were slumping. It was the holiday season, and his sales were actually decreasing! Something had to be done.

Murphey hired a marketing consultant to brainstorm some ideas to generate more sales. He hired JP Maroney who came up with a powerful idea. Maroney convinced Murphey to send faxes to business owners in his city. The fax offered the business owner or manager $50 gift certificates to provide to all of his employees as a holiday gift or end-of-year bonus. The business owner just had to call Murphey and tell him his company name and the number of employees he had. Murphey would give him gift certificates for all his employees. On top of that, Murphey would also give away a $100 gift certificate to the business owner. This provided an added incentive to the business owner to call Murphey and ask for the gift certificates!

This fax campaign worked wonders. Within 4 days, 74 business owners called Murphey and requested gift certificates for 3,127 employees! How could Murphey afford to give away $50 gift certificates to 3,127 people? Simple. Murphey realizes that a product worth $50 at retail price costs him just $17 at wholesale and most people would buy a jewelry piece worth much more than $50 when they use the certificate. In fact, Murphey's calculations showed that the average invoice amount per sale is over $200! And the lifetime value per client is over $2500 on average! Further calculations show that if only 20% of people used the gift certificates, and became lifetime clients, Murphey would make $1.56 million dollars! Such stellar results just because of a $90 fax promotion!

Action Summary:

- You could copy this exact strategy. You could contact business owners and make them an offer to give away your gift certificates to their employees. Most people save gift certificates for a long time. If you want quicker results, you could add a deadline to that gift certificate (e.g., make the gift certificates valid only till May 31st).

- Gift certificates could be a cheap way to bring people to your store and make a purchase. Once they are happy with their purchase, they will keep on coming back to you.

- Calculate your average sale and the lifetime value of a client to determine the value of gift certificates you can afford to give away.

Winning the Seasonal Wars

Some businesses have seasonal ups and downs. One such business is that of a lawn service provider. Business is good in summers. But during winters, no one buys lawn servicing, bringing a cash flow problem to the business. A bad summer can mean doom for the small business owner!

One lawn servicing business tried to change its winter blues by starting a winter promotion program. They sent brochures to people by mail. They explained that in summers, the lawn service providers are usually busy and so by signing a contract in winter, they would lock in the service for summer. To increase the number of people who would sign the contracts in winter, they promised a bribe. Anyone who signed the contract before a certain date would receive a beautiful embroidered blanket!

This simple tactic helped the lawn servicing business over its winter lull and it also increased their business by 40% more than other similar lawn service providers get over the year!

Action Summary:

- Advertise when others aren't advertising.
- You don't have to provide the product now to make the sale. You can make the sale and promise to provide the product at a later date. Getting people to sign contracts in the winter meant that the competition wouldn't get the contracts in the summer!
- Provide an incentive, a bonus, or a bribe to get people to act now!

Free Wine Anyone?

Jack wanted to get more locals to visit his restaurants. So he employed one simple marketing tactic. He spent $1,625 in one year on the marketing tactic and that tactic received a 29% response and brought in $106,177 in revenue. What was it?

Sending congratulatory notes to people who were featured in newspapers; Jack hired an administrator who would read news for 45 minutes every day and find people who were just promoted. He would then find their contact information, and send a personalized letter to them offering free wine.

This simple tactic was a great hit. The personalized letter didn't only receive a 29% response rate, but each person who came to the restaurant due to the letter revisited the restaurant an average of 3 times in one year! Every dollar spent on the marketing tactic brought in more than $65 in revenue!

Action Summary:

- Give away freebies to your target audience to attract them to your store.
- Personalize your offer for the best response.
- Look in the newspaper or online for people to target.

Niche

Not to be confused with Nietzsche

Niching is a technique that has been around for a long time. It can change the landscape of a product overnight. To niche or not to niche, that is the question. There are some dangers associated with niching. It takes some planning, and consequences must be weighed. You are stepping away from the mainstream. You are purposely leaving the bulk of the common target audience in order to dominate a larger percentage of a smaller audience. It is the target audience because for years it has probably yielded the most results for that product. If you are in a market that is saturated by competitors that vary only slightly, niching yourself and owning a piece of the pie completely may be more financially rewarding than fighting for a percentage of the whole pie. This has been done a number of times successfully.

There were a number of cold medications fighting for the largest market share of the "cold medicine users" pie. A new medicine shows up and says, "We don't want to fight all those companies for a piece of that pie; let's just be the nighttime guys." They gave up the whole pie to own a piece. That year, Nyquil became the "nighttime, sniffling, sneezing, coughing, aching, stuffy-head, fever, so you can rest medicine."

They ended up shifting the market by changing how people perceived the medicine pie. Companies that owned giant shares of the "cold medicine users" pie woke up the next morning with a smaller piece of the market, because their pie was split into daytime and nighttime medicine users, and they didn't have a share of the nighttime half. Is that the story of how it happened or why? Probably not, but it is the result on the consumer's end and, in marketing, that's the important part.

Jim Doyle, of Jim Doyle and Associates, is one of the most successful television consultants in the industry today. He works with television sales staffs and their clients on a daily basis to help them come up with better strategies for their commercials. Niching is a technique that Jim can tell countless stories about. He has had phenomenal success with it a number of times. He can tell you stories of a last-place car dealer who decided to niche and become the "Truck King" and within a short period of time, moved into one of the top spots in his market. Jim Doyle helps companies niche on a local level, so you don't have to be a giant in a giant category to succeed. You just have to have the conviction to change your way of thinking and take a risk.

Niching can shift a market completely or possibly bring a new customer to the table as in the story of "Ranch Candles." Vicky made the most wonderful-smelling candles and they could fill a room with a scent in a matter of minutes. She wasn't into making a huge profit as she had a day job and this was just her night hobby. This was a company that just wasn't positioned for growth even though they had a superior product.

One evening a frantic knock came at the door. A young college-aged girl entered and asked, "How many of those candles do you have left?" There were five and she bought all five and grabbed the box. When she was asked what the deal was, she said that her boyfriend and his friends were over the night before and they were smoking. She just received a call from her mother who was coming into town and the candles were the only things she knew that would get rid of the smell.

Who knew that these candles covered up the smell of weed? (I do not agree with illegal drug use...it's just part of the story – ok mom?) It covered the odors up enough that I had an idea.

I remember being in college and there were five boys living in a house. We probably went through more candles than any of the girls we went to school with. If we walked into a room and it smelled funny, instead of doing the responsible thing and doing the laundry or finding the hot wing that fell on the floor and rolled under the couch, we would light a candle to cover up the smell. But we used to pick on each other due to the feminine names. With a Web page design drawn on a napkin and an evening of laughing it up and coming up with ideas, Wakwix.com was born.

"There comes a time in every boy's life when he has to step boldly into manhood. This step includes babes, beers, booze and buddies...sometimes body hair growth. It is a time to leave behind the childhood things of yesteryear. Goodbye to mom's home cooking, goodbye laundry waiting folded by the bed, goodbye to someone cleaning up behind you. Hello to independence, fast food, paper plates and unwanted odors.

Face it boys, cleanliness isn't always our thing. To mask these odors some of us resort to cleaning and scrubbing, washing and wiping, dusting and polishing. For the other 97 percent, we buy candles. They are classy, sophisticated, romantic and they get rid of the smells. If you go to any retail outlet and look at a candle to purchase, you will run into a dilemma. They are all named 'soft meadow,' 'angel fresh' and 'peach blossom.' Herein lies the problem. Just imagine rocking out to some heavy metal, kicking back some cold ones, telling stories about hot ones and you ask your boy to light up a 'soft angel blossom' candle. Yep, I see them hog-tying you and trying to find a dress in your size. That's where we come in.

It's time for a candle that can both cover up all sorts of smells and let you keep your manliness at the same time. So from all of us at wakwix - enjoy the manhood and leave the covering up of smells to us. Our slogan is 'good smell.' It was gonna be 'protecting your sissy ass from being forced to wear a dress' but it didn't flow as well."

You can visit Wakwix.com on the Internet and enjoy the wonderful scents of powerful candles but they will be under the WakWix names of

"Weed-Be-Gone," "Hello Officer," "Dirty Laundry Fresh," "Pooh-Be-Gone" and "Smells Like We Cleaned," and believe me, it will cover up all sorts of smells. For full disclosure, I am now a major share holder in this company. That's how much I enjoyed this story.

To niche, it is important to look at your business category and see if it is a risk you are willing to take. There are just as many companies that niched themselves out of business as were successful. Then you need to find out which audience isn't your current target audience and see if you could convince them to buy as in the Wakwix case or if you can change the way they use your product like in the Nyquil example. You don't want to niche so small that you don't have much of an audience, or niche yourself into another dominated category.

Beware the Niche

Dave purchased a vitamin and whole foods company that was in business for years. He was a shopper there for a long time and was the first person contacted when it went up for sale. His interest was in bodybuilding and he was very knowledgeable. When he took the store over, he started changing what it was known for. He started carrying more weightlifting supplements and less of the things the store historically kept in inventory. When we spoke, he said that he wanted to niche to the bodybuilding crowd.

In a town of one hundred thousand, with two bodybuilding stores already in business, was this a smart move? Out of the three stores, he was easily the most educated owner but he niched so small, into an already saturated market. He was also using a name that was synonymous with a different product. He didn't have the marketing dollars that it was going to take to completely change the market's perception of his store, and overcome the already established stores' reputations.

The company was soon out of business. If he had continued to run the company in the manner in which it had been successful, he may have been better off opening a sister location that targeted bodybuilding.

Action Summary:

- Niching is a dangerous strategy; it's not a fix-all.
- To niche or not to niche, that is the question.
- It's hard to break away from known history.
- Niching too small can be deadly.

The Magical Laundry Lady

Half a century ago, a lady started a laundry service. She was brilliant, magical even. She could take out everything from coffee stains to mud to even pet stains. She had a bag full of tricks to remove any and every type of stain. Her venture was quite successful. Clients were becoming loyal and used to come back to her week after week.

Soon her reputation spread far and wide. She could no longer handle all the work she got. So she decided to restrict her services only to one group of people. She changed tracks and started a "laundry service for bachelors only."

Something really strange happened. Her strategy backfired. She started receiving more work than ever before! When she restricted her services to one target audience, she differentiated herself from laundry services. Every bachelor in town started coming to her for their laundry needs.

What's more, because of her unique service, she received loads of free publicity and bachelors from nearby towns brought their business to her too.

Action Summary:

- You can differentiate your product by targeting one audience.
- It can be more profitable to target a large piece of a smaller cake than a small piece of a larger cake.
- By targeting one audience, you will position yourself as a specialist for the service you provide.
- Market to a smaller niche audience and you will earn more.

Selling Bulbs With a Twist

It was the fall of 1987. Steve had just been fired from his software design firm. Steve read about halogen light bulbs in the International Design Yearbook and he saw a huge potential in the market for halogen lamps. He and his wife decided to start selling the halogen lamps.

Then the real troubles began. They soon found out that it wasn't that easy to sell the halogen lamps. Without much money to spend on advertisements, it was even harder. They placed a few classified ads in magazines promoting how good the halogen lamps looked. But the results weren't good. They received only about 5 responses to their first ad. Not sales, but responses. The results were quite disheartening.

They were about to give in to fate when "light bulbs" went on in their brains. They realized that they could go after the market with different bait. They realized that the appeal for the halogen lamps was not only their good looks, but their effectiveness too.

They placed a 1-inch ad and their destinies changed. They started getting loads of responses. They started converting those responses into sales. Their profits soared. Today they both are millionaires! The ad?

"Serious Light for Serious Readers!"

Action Summary:

- Selling to a target market brings in a better response than trying to sell to everyone.
- Focusing on a different attribute of the product can bring in better results too. They focused on the effectiveness of the halogen lamps while everyone else was focusing on their good looks.

Barrier Marketing

B. T. is one of the many wealth management and private investment companies in America. They offer various services like asset management, estate administration, and overlooking stock exchange investments. They tried to find new clients the same way other private investment bankers did: cold calling.

They'd hired sales representatives to cold call doctors, dentists, small business owners and everyone else who would want to hire professionals for wealth management and investment help.

B. T. was making good money, but nothing out of the ordinary. They had a few very wealthy clients who were very profitable. But most of their clients didn't invest a lot and not all of them were even profitable for the company.

After a really bad quarter, one day, the executives sat down together and brainstormed: "If we have to spend the same amount of time to manage money for wealthy and profitable clients as for not-so-wealthy and unprofitable clients, why don't we only work the ones that are more profitable?"

The next day, they started firing most of their clients. They erected a barrier: they would take on a person as their client only if he or she had $5 million in assets to manage. Even though their number of clients decreased and the workload reduced, they didn't fire any of their employees. As a result, the few bigger clients they had started receiving a lot more attention and better service. They attracted very few new clients in the beginning.

Soon, the word started to spread about their $5 million barrier and their top service. Now, instead of cold calling and chasing clients, prospects chase B. T. to see if they can become clients.

Action Summary:

- ■ Erect barriers. Don't work with everyone. Choose your clients well. You'll attract more of them.
- ■ Remember: the type of clients you handle represents you. If you handle shady clients, you'll receive more shady work.
- ■ If you work with top clients only, you'll attract more clients like them.

Billion $ Bank vs. Trillion $ Banks

A bank in New York, Sterling National Bank, had 2 billion dollars in assets. That would be monumental in most businesses, but it was considered insignificant for New York banks, where Citigroup and J.P. Morgan Chase have more than a trillion dollars in assets – each.

In 1992, Sterling National Bank was in a quandary. The first and only chairman they'd had till then died. The new management had to make a decision: take the easy way and find a bigger bank to buy them out, or to take the hard way and fight and grow against stiff competition. The new management decided to take the hard way!

Sterling National Bank realized that with their limited resources, they couldn't compete against the big banks on all fronts. So they decided to focus on one niche only. They decided to stop pursuing consumer banking. They also avoided going after big business banking. Instead, Sterling started focusing on the unglamorous small business lending. They targeted business loans in the range of $500,000 to $15 million.

Sterling decided to be the best in their niche. While other banks were cutting costs by automating things that reduced the personal touch, Sterling emphasized providing personal service, even if that meant higher costs. Sterling even threw out the voice automation system, and every caller would receive a real person instead of voice mail on the other end when they called!

Sterling started hosting lunch sessions where small groups of borrowers were invited to mingle with the top executives of the bank. The bank executives could thus have their fingers on the pulse of the market and keep ahead of trends and problems. Sterling did everything possible to help their clients. They even started giving credit for courses on real estate and other topics.

These personal touches meant that Sterling had to charge a quarter percent point higher interest rate than their competitors. But their clients didn't mind the higher costs because of the personal services they received. In fact, Sterling is such a hit among small business owners that they saw their 43rd consecutive quarter of double-digit growth in earnings!

Action Summary:

- Narrow your target audience. Don't go after everyone.
- Provide better services. People will pay a higher rate for your products and services if they receive a better experience from you.
- Add the personal touch. Personal Experience Factor!
- Meet with your top clients occasionally and listen to them, their problems, and their wants. Inviting your clients to lunch is the cheapest market research you can do effectively.

Selling to Locksmiths

Danna ran a software company. She and her team developed a quick and easy Rolodex software. People could scan the business cards they received and add them to the software. They could search among hundreds of them easily when required. But the competition was intense. There were quite a few software options on the market already. A few of them were more famous than Danna's software. So she decided to focus on smaller markets.

She chose locksmiths as her first market. She customized the software with a few added features that locksmiths would want and removed a few features that would be of no use for locksmiths. Then she renamed the software "Locksmith's Handy Rolodex" and started selling it online.

Then one day, she put on her thinking cap and brainstormed on how she could sell hundreds of copies of software together. She came up with a brilliant idea. She went to a few locksmith schools and gave away her software copies for free.

Soon, the schools were using her software to teach other locksmiths how they could use it effectively to grow their business. After graduation, many of those new locksmiths bought Danna's software. Danna then went to locksmith associations and gave away free copies to them too. The association gave away these copies of her software to a few people during meetings and mentioned the software in their newsletters. Soon, almost all the locksmiths were using Danna's software. Danna then shifted her focus to the medical industry and repeated her success.

Action Summary:

- When the competition is too intense, niche. Focus on a smaller target audience. You'll do much better by being a big fish in a small pond than by being a small fish in a big pond.
- Give away a few units of your products to the influencers. Determine who your target audience is. Then figure out who they listen to. Then contact these people and give them free samples and offers. If your product is good, these people will talk about it.
- Be careful. If your product isn't good and you give it away to key influentials, they will talk about that too.

The Potato King

During the 1930's Great Depression in America, there lived a young man named John who ran a salad business from a small store. John made all sorts of salads with various ingredients, packaged them and sold them to restaurants. But when the Depression came, it hit him hard and many restaurants stopped buying his salads.

Cutting down costs, John started making only one kind of salad: potato salad. Then John did something very unusual and something that many said was plain stupid. Many advised John to make lower-cost potato salad that people could buy as a substitute for a meal during hard times. Instead, John added fancy ingredients to the salad and made it a luxury potato salad. He added only the finest ingredients, and tried to sell it to the local restaurants.

The sales were slow to come, as restaurant owners didn't think it was a wise idea to sell expensive salads anymore. But the public surprised the restaurant owners too, by demanding John's expensive potato salad. To meet the public demand, many local restaurants and delicatessens lined up to buy the potato salads from John. Business became so good that John had to hire more staff to cut and mix potatoes.

While other salad makers focused on making their salads more affordable to the average person, John went the other way and gave people a product they could indulge in during the Depression. As a result, John became the king of potato salad!

Action Summary:

- Focus down and find a niche to grow your business. When John decided to make only potato salads, his business grew and when people thought of potato salads, they thought of John.
- Go against the norm. If you zag when everyone zigs, you'll make a name for yourself earning a lot more money.

Firing Clients

Dr. Randy is a dentist. He hit hard times. Insurance agencies stopped covering standard procedures, which led to a decline in the number of patients. On top of that, better toothpaste technology led to a decline in cavity rates, further hurting Dr. Randy's practice and if that wasn't enough, more and more students were graduating from dentistry school, which generated a glut of dentists.

Competition was really intense and Dr. Randy realized that he had to do something really soon. So back to school he went. Dr. Randy signed up for classes at the Las Vegas Institute for Advanced Dental Studies – a school known for cosmetic dentistry. Dr. Randy then plugged in whitening and other elective procedural devices and positioned himself as a dentist who specializes in cosmetic dentistry. He started taking on people who wanted better smiles. After that, Dr. Randy gave his office a makeover. He adorned the office walls with large photos of patients with million-dollar smiles and played classical music in the waiting room. He even made sure that the air didn't smell like a normal dentist office. Air fresheners gave the offices a pleasant smell.

That done Dr. Randy fired some of his clients. He stopped accepting insurance and cut down the number of appointments per day, yet made a lot more money than ever before. In his own words: "We shifted from needs-based dentistry to wants-based dentistry. It has totally transformed our practice and our personal lives. We see a much smaller number of patients, at a slower pace." Yet he makes much more money.

Action Summary:

■ Keep on educating yourself. Learn the new methods and techniques in your industry and then implement them.

- Specialize. Focus on a particular segment of your industry. Or target a specific audience. Focus on the people who make good clients. Fire everyone else.
- Instead of being a small fish in a big pond, try to be a big fish in a small pond and your profits will increase.
- Start focusing on what people want, instead of what people need. Your business will boom.

Deuce! Selling Sunglasses

Some 30 years back, K.E. manufactured sunglasses. His sunglasses were of good quality and they were cool-looking, too. But the other big branded companies always sold more units than him. K.E. didn't have much money to advertise his top-quality sunglasses and thus he could never successfully create awareness about his cool-looking and longer-lasting sunglasses.

So he targeted a smaller market. He went after athletes. He saw an instant rise in sales as his marketing effort became more focused and word of his sunglasses started spreading among the athletes.

And then K.E. did one more thing that made the sales jump an awesome 34% in one single year: he started packaging the sunglasses in tennis ball cans! The unique packaging spread the word about his sunglasses like wildfire and he could now charge more as he positioned his sunglasses as cool. His profits exploded.

Action Summary:

- Targeting a smaller market often leads to more profits as now your marketing material is focused on one audience and pulls in a better response.

- Unique packaging alone has the potential to jump-start your sales. Unique packaging will make people talk about your product. It will make them remember your product.
- With the combined power of packaging and smart targeting, you can easily increase your prices without seeing any decline in sales.

No Pets Allowed?

Most apartment complexes don't allow pets. Pets make a mess. The common areas in the apartment complexes need constant cleaning due to the pets and on top of that, some pets can be a nuisance if their owners can't handle them. If a dog staying in a house barks during the night, he'll only wake up the people who stay in the house. But if a dog staying in an apartment barks during the night, the entire apartment complex will wake up and usually, when one dog starts barking, all the other dogs in the vicinity start barking too.

People with pets understand if something like this happens. But people staying in the same complex who don't have pets complain. For such reasons, most apartment complexes have a strict "No Pets Allowed" policy. You can be chucked out of your apartment if you break the rule. So it was noteworthy when one apartment complex bucked the trend. One apartment complex in Colorado proudly published an ad in the papers that read in bold: "Pets Required!"

They made it obligatory for their residents to have pets! Reading that ad, pet owners and lovers flocked to that apartment complex. The apartment complex charged more rent than the neighboring complex, yet it was booked full in no time. In fact, their rule was so successful; they had a waiting list of people who wanted to stay in the complex.

Action Summary:

- Buck the trend. Do what your competition isn't doing. Do what your competition is afraid of doing. Zag when your competition zigs.
- Qualify your clients with a condition. Focus on a target audience and only do business with one group of people, and you'll have more business than people who do business with anyone and everyone.
- Pay special attention to any laws that might affect your business category.

Bald is Beautiful

Gary has a good life. He lives in a small town and owns a restaurant and bar. Now Gary is bald, and he used that as an opportunity. He changed the world and made baldness trendy.

Gary waited a few weeks to see how his restaurant did on different days of the week. He found out that Wednesdays were the slowest days. Gary then started a Wednesday promotion: "Bald people eat free on Wednesdays!"

A totally hairless head will fetch a diner a completely free meal. Diners with less than 50 percent of their hair get up to 50 percent off their food. It didn't matter if diners went bald naturally or shaved off their heads. Diners paid according to the amount of hair on their heads on Wednesdays.

The news of "Bald people eat free on Wednesdays" reached far and wide. Gary's uptown restaurant and bar has received tons of free publicity because of the promotional tactic. The restaurant was featured in newspapers published in as far away places as London.

This eat-free promotional tactic doubled the business on

Wednesdays and converted it from one of the slowest days into one of the fastest.

"We haven't had a single bald guy dine alone. One hairless fellow brought five women with him," said Gary.

Action Summary:

- You could start such a promotion too. Select a group of people you want to reward and then make a special offer to them.
- For example: Baby boomers can have 5% off on Tuesdays. Government employees can receive a free goodie.
- Then announce the offer through press releases and advertising.

A company must establish how it is going to do business. Opening the doors without a plan is like walking onto the field of battle without having looked at the map. Very often "doing it the way it has always been done" is just an excuse not to rock the boat or take on a challenge, because change is challenging. It can also be ridiculously rewarding. Many of the ideas here carry a large risk, but didn't going into business in the first place take just as much risk? Try change on a smaller scale like Monica's Hair Membership or try marketing a specific day, like "Bald Wednesdays".

Realize that there will always be naysayers and those who are afraid to change. I'm sure that this is the same type of resistance that Henry Ford met when he said, "I have a theory on how we can make a lot of cars, really fast!"

The World of the Customer

Section Three

A company, once it establishes how it is going to do business, must market itself to the outside world. The owners must learn how the world sees not only their business but their industry as well. Once it is known what is important to the customer, it is vital to market your business with those desires in mind.

Tet Offensive (Brainstorm)

Without going into a huge history lesson filled with many facts and figures, I am going to touch on a moment during the Vietnam conflict known as the Tet Offensive. It will be a brief and shallow glance at this historical event.

The ideas behind the planning of the Tet Offensive help to lay a methodology for planning "Business Marketing."

The US had fought wars against large armies. The guerilla warfare methods of the N. Vietnamese, also known as the Vietcong (VC), were different than our way of fighting wars. The VC could not fight the war the way the US wanted them to fight. They had to focus their energies in places that they could.

The US wasn't doing a wonderful job winning the hearts of the villagers in the rural parts of the country. The VC made it a major effort to build positive relations with the villagers. During the Tet holiday, the villagers would be instrumental in sneaking the weapons in for the battle.

Back in the United States, the government was telling the people that the US was dominantly in control. There were protests going on back in the states. If the VC could show that they were not as defeated as the press was saying, it could turn the tide politically. So, the Tet offensive began with the North Vietnamese army capturing locations that had no military value. There were many little victories that didn't amount to too much militarily. However, the United States media captured all of the little skirmishes.

Everyone sitting back at home saw all these battles breaking out. How could a dominant US military allow so many attacks to be happening? The public opinion decided that we weren't winning as much as we claimed to be. This created a political problem for the president and the tide turned towards ending the Vietnam conflict. The Tet Offensive, while offering no real military advantage to the North Vietnamese, is considered the event that started the failure of the American support for the war at home, thus leading to the eventual withdrawal of the American troops.

There is a marketing lesson to learn here. We have to answer a few different questions:

- *Are there some battles that we are just not going to be able to win?*
- *Just because something has always been done that way, does it mean we have to continue doing it that way?*
- *Are there some customers that are being under-serviced or under-appreciated who might open up an opportunity?*
- *Is there another way to win the marketing battle?*
- *Are there any political gains that might be made?*
- *Are there different wars that can be won, other than the obvious ones?*

When you start looking at the industry and the business and ask these questions, using the Tet Offensive as the basis, many new ideas can be born from the methodology.

Turd in the Punchbowl
"With a chapter title like that, who needs witty banter in the subtitle?"

My goal wasn't necessarily to offend anyone with the title of this little chapter. The purpose was to get your attention. Ironically, that is the purpose of the "Turd in the Punchbowl" technique. Tell people what they already know but aren't saying. If the customer knows that you are real, then they feel like they can trust you when it comes to services or products. What is the underlying truth about your industry or your specific situation?

Sometimes it's amazing what answers you will get when you try to find out what displeases people about your industry. Allstate Insurance ran an ad campaign discussing some of these items in the auto industry. They "dropped the turd in the punchbowl." Don't you hate how you can be a fantastic driver for years and with one accident, your premium goes up? What about if your premium went down if you didn't have an accident instead of just up when you do?

I have personally had these conversations with friends in the past. It was almost like Allstate asked one of us what irritated us about their industry and then brought it up in their advertising, and offered a solution.

Fun Dentist?

Dr. Wiley knew that a dentist's office isn't the type of place that a mother likes to bring her child, especially if she has more than one. Well, if having a kid-friendly office would allow for more mothers to make appointments, it couldn't be a bad thing to do.

"We know going to the dentist isn't fun; heck, if they didn't pay us, we wouldn't come in here, but we know how important good tooth

care is. So in an attempt to make the trip to the dentist a bit more fun, Dr. Wiley has brought his X-Box 360 up and purchased a 52" Wide screen TV. The office also has Wireless Internet access in case you want to bring some of your work with you to keep you occupied. Give us a bit of your time, have some fun and make sure that your teeth and gums are healthy enough that you only have to visit us once a year."

Dr. Wiley knows that people don't like the dentist but instead of trying to hide this fact, he goes straight at it. He says it himself. The humor in his ads, and the solutions he offers for parents to make the dentist a bit more fun for their children have his appointments filled solid for weeks out, and customers looking forward to visiting the dentist.

Action Summary:

- ■ This is an example of saying what people are already saying, and trying to offer a solution.
- ■ Is this the perfect idea for every dentist? Not likely. Dr. Wiley gave up some specific customers by going this direction.
- ■ It's important to look at the situation of the market and the current clients before you do this specific strategy, but one could be tailored to fit almost any business.

Great Food, Bad Spot!

Sandoval's Restaurant had a problem. It had great food but a terrible location. It was out of the way, off the beaten path, and every other person said, "why'd you put your restaurant there?" A number of restaurants had made attempts at succeeding at this location but didn't make it. Sandoval's Restaurant had an idea how to avoid the fate of the previous restaurants. They were going to talk about the "curse" and having a bad location openly.

"Why didn't someone tell us that we are the 5th restaurant in as many years to go into this location? At Sandoval's, we have world famous chefs preparing meals that you can expect to get in fine European restaurants around the world. Fine dining? Contest-winning food? Incredible wait staff? Great Wine selection? We do all of this well, obviously picking real estate isn't one of our areas of expertise. But, for a little drive to a slightly out of the way 'cursed' location…we will defy the odds because after one visit, we will have you coming back for more. Come to potentially the worst location for the best meal…Sandovals."

It was a stroke of genius when they talked about it in their advertising, even making jokes about the owner knowing how to cook, but not knowing how to pick real estate. Everyone always said it was a "cursed location" because no other restaurant made it there, but these people had the guts to drop the turd in the punchbowl and open a discussion about it. It became something that people joked about, but they visited the location.

Action Summary:

- Is there something about your company, industry, location or team that is hurting your business? Can you bring light to it by actually discussing it?
- In talking about your shortcomings, you prevent competitors from doing it and you seem real to your customers.
- Be honest with your customers.

■ If you don't know where there are areas you can improve, ask
    your customers and friends about your industry as a whole, not
    just your company.

Build a Community
"Come, drink the Kool-aid and get on the Comet!"

It makes sense to go after the largest number of sales that you possibly can. Twistavants Candles in Lubbock, Texas has the most incredibly strong-smelling candles. Jon and Eve Avent sell many of them right out of their store, but they will tell you that a bulk of the money comes from the flower shops, bakeries and school fund raisers that move their product in bulk.

One way to increase the amount of product you sell is to create a community. The Avents created a community of vendors. There are many ways to create a community, but once one has been established, all of them lead to increased profits and great word of mouth. Just ask anyone who has ever lit a Twistavants candle. (Twistavants.com)

Selling More Flour – One Pound at a Time

King Arthur Flour Company is based in Vermont, USA. It's a 200-year-old company that had failed to grow with time. Up until 1993, King Arthur flour was available in only 11 of the 50 states in America.

King Arthur Flour wasn't much different than other flours. After all, how different can flour be? Maybe that was one of the reasons for its stagnation. But in the last 5 years, King Arthur flour did a complete turnaround. Last year, sales grew by 20%! How?

King Arthur started building a community. In the year 2000, they sent an email to 40,000 of their customers asking them to join bakingcircle.com – an online community. Members could now swap recipes, ask questions and post answers, and upload pictures of baked food.

The community was a wild success. In less than 4 years, it grew 50-fold. The King Arthur catalog now hits 9 million homes, and King Arthur flour made it to supermarkets in all 50 states. The company has a team of 100,000 loyal evangelists who spread the word and as a result, sales grew by an awesome 20% since last year alone.

Action Summary:

- Build a community. A community can help you convert one-time buyers into loyal buyers.
- Members of bakingcircle.com buy directly from King Arthur. Not only that, they buy three times more often than non-members. And if that wasn't enough, they also spend $12 more on each order! A community makes people buy more stuff from you more often.

Chinatown Plaza

Mr. Chen had a dream. He wanted to build America's first "planned" China Town in Las Vegas. But there were huge obstacles to overcome before his ambitious dream could come true. The main one was this: Only about 10,000 Chinese lived in the state of Nevada. Unlike San Francisco and other coastal cities, they were not as concentrated within a certain neighborhood.

To test his dream, Mr. Chen opened a Chinese video store. The video store didn't earn him much, but he did collect the zip codes of other Asians living in Nevada. He mapped out where they lived.

Armed with his zip code data, Mr. Chen zeroed in on a new development complex where many Asians were buying houses. With his partners, he bought 8 acres of land near the development. He built "Chinatown Plaza" - a shopping center especially targeting the Asian lifestyle and culture. It became wildly successful. Many people started coming to the shopping center from far away. They would spend a whole day in the shopping center. It was like a picnic.

His shopping center is so successful that today competitors are developing 2 other similar shopping centers for the Asian community nearby.

Action Summary:

- Testing! Test the viability of your product before you roll out with it in full force. You can save a lot of money by testing your product and analyzing whether the market demands it or not.
- Collect information from your prospective audience. If you know where they live, you can use it to your advantage and open your shop at a good location.
- If you know their habits, you can customize your marketing material.

Slogan Tie

"I think they are singing our song"

Somewhere in the country right now, someone is on their cell phone with their head cocked to the side with one finger on the antennae saying "Can you hear me, can you hear me now?" At the same time this is happening, a man is coming up for a speech in front of a large audience and grabbing the microphone. Instead of saying, "Testing, one, two, three," he is chanting the slogan for Verizon Wireless: "Can you hear me, can you hear me now?" and it is being met with laughter from the crowd and for Verizon, this was marketing gold.

The technique that they so sweetly scored with is called the slogan tie. Find something common in your industry and tie your slogan to it. Other household phrases that usually were followed by a product plug were "Pardon me," almost always followed with "Do you have any Grey Poupon?" When you hear "Give me a break," do you start humming the Kit Kat song? "Give me a break, give me a break, break me off a piece of that Kit Kat Bar." You are probably humming the song now. In fact, just after writing that, I will probably be humming it for the rest of the night. Let's not forget "Who you gonna call … Ghostbusters?" While it wasn't a product, it was a phrase that brought a specific brand to mind.

How many times an evening are the phrases "What do you want for dinner?" or "Where do you want to go?" uttered? How much would it be worth to a company to have their name screamed by the kids in the car every time their parents said that, even if they were just finishing the slogan? That doesn't mean that every time that restaurant would win, but how often would it be thrown on the table as an option? That would be a fantastic place to be sitting in the mind of the customer.

To use the Slogan Tie technique, make sure it is a statement that is pertinent to your business and something that a person might say when they are in the market to buy your product. A nice jingle or pitch person would be good to help push the marketing. Make sure to get the frequency in; you need to make sure that this becomes an automatic thought when the catchphrase is heard. It takes time to do this and it requires all your marketing across the board to include this same theme. You will have to continue with this theme for a while. Change your copy but keep the same theme. Make sure the theme is catchy and make sure the phrase is common enough to get repetition or definitely pertains to your product enough that the few times it is said, listeners are surely in the market for your product type.

This technique is very rewarding but also can be annoying. The business owner is tying their company to a single phrase, possibly for life. When it works, though, this kind of marketing is Priceless. MasterCard anyone?

Burger Doodle

During the 1950's in West Fargo, there was a large national restaurant that ran a commercial discussing the quality of their food. They described the agony of going to the grocery store and having to cook and clean, or sitting and eating in your car at the "Burger Doodle" and praised the ease and joy you would experience when eating at their sit-down restaurant. Who knows how that worked? It was back in the 50's and the story would have ended there. But since it's in a case study, you know it didn't!

There in West Fargo was a drive-in restaurant where you did eat in the car. You would consider it similar to the Sonic Drive-Ins of today. They saw a moment and capitalized on it. They changed their name to "Burger Doodle". The national chain was pushing their commercial so heavily that it became funny to actually eat at the

"Burger Doodle" in your car. Word of mouth exploded and a fictional drive in restaurant that was given birth in a commercial, grew up and made a killing, back in the 50's, in a town called West Fargo.

Action Summary:

- ■ Listen to the advertising of your competition.
- ■ Sometimes it will open up a door for you to waltz through.
- ■ It's OK to be outrageous.

Hero-ify

There you go again, always causing problems!

Jeff is the owner of a family-owned jewelry store. His company was well established in the community, as it had been there for over 100 years. It was THE quality place to go if you were looking for anything from wedding rings to birthday gifts. He was more expensive than the mall and the large retail outlet jewelry stores, but that was his niche, quality and personal service.

Jeff told me his marketing dilemma was how to get a middle-aged guy to want to buy something for his girl. He was after the sales that should come after the engagement ring; the middle of a relationship buys. He wants to sell the bracelets and watches and rings as well. He had to create a problem and offer his company as the Hero.

My girlfriend and I had been dating for over a year at this time and I was crazy for her. She and I would hug and kiss and hold hands at any occasion. We always gave each other "butterflies" when we would see each other. You know the kind of butterflies I am talking about, the light fluttering in your abdomen when you think of that special someone. Young love at its finest. Bambi's twitterpated if you will. We have all been there and we have all talked about the butterflies. She asked me that day at lunch, "Do you think we will still get butterflies ten years from now?" And of course I responded, "I know we will!" because I believed it! Even if I didn't believe it, I would have said yes to avoid getting forked. I know how important these butterflies are to her. Imagine if she and I were riding in the car ten years from now and this radio ad came on:

"From the first kiss to the one millionth kiss, if she still gives you butterflies, show her with a gift from so-and-so Jewelers!"

Could you imagine the change in that car? Minutes before, I was fine; one commercial later, the comfy world I was used to now hangs in jeopardy. I now teetered on the brink of sleeping on the couch, finding my own meals and figuring out how to iron. My simple life has been disturbed, all because I hadn't mentioned the butterflies in a while. Thanks to that commercial, my only source of salvation is quickly getting to the jewelry store, signing up for a credit card and spending till it hurts. Nothing had really changed. The problem of "not mentioning butterflies" was there the whole time. It just took the commercial to point it out.

To use hero-ifying, look to see what kind of problems could exist that your business can solve. Then let people know that a problem exists, for most of the time people are accepting of problems because they believe it is just the way things are. Many times, they don't know an option is available. Create the problem and then offer a solution.

Bowling the Competitors Out

Bowling is a game whose peak has come and gone. It saw its peak in 1970s when the bowling leagues had 4.5 million bowlers. Today, fewer than half that number remain!

Even though the bowling craze has subsided, the competition for selling bowling balls is intense. There are quite a few companies that make these balls and sell them through many gaming stores. Even though the competition was intense, Bill Chrisman wasn't deterred. He had a passion for bowling and wanted to sell his own bowling balls.

But how to get people to buy his bowling balls over the others? Bill couldn't make his product better or even color them brighter, because all the other competitors had already done that. So how could Bill break away from the competition and become the market leader?

Bill did something that no one had ever thought of. He used the power of smell to make his bowling balls stand out from the crowd. He started selling scented bowling balls through the pro game shops! How did Bill get the idea to come up with scented balls in the first place?

I'll let him answer that:

"Most of the pro shops were very small. I'm not going to say they had a bad odor to them, but they were kind of musty," says Bill. "I thought if we put in a fragrance, people would go over and smell the balls, touch the balls, and read our name on the balls."

Apparently his idea worked, and within 5 years, people are paying a premium to buy balls that smell like banana, French fries, and 100 other fragrances!

Action Summary:

- The problem of the bad smell was always there. Bill's just offering his company as the hero.
- Smell is one of the most ignored factors in product manufacturing (except in candles). People work on size, shape and color of their products. But they forget about smell. You could give a fragrance to your products and take the market lead.
- You could make your shop stand out from other shops in the locality by making it smell good.
- Don't forget that people have 5 main senses that help them feel a certain way about a product: touch, sight, sound, smell and taste.
- Make use of all five of them if you can.

Error-Free Banks

A few decades back, when computers weren't that prevalent in banks, a bank came out with a simple marketing campaign that knocked their local competitors out. They ran an ad in the local newspaper that asked people to join their bank. But they didn't offer a lower rate on borrowings, and neither did they pay a higher interest rate on savings than other banks did. They simply offered people a challenge:

"Find any error in the monthly statement and receive $10 for each error!"

By making this offer, the bank made people believe that their accounting system was safer than their competitors, and they would keep people's money safe. In all reality, their system wasn't any different than the other local banks. But because they were the first to make such an offer, they received a flood of new clients. A little more than 12,000 people opened their accounts with this bank, and brought in about 65 million dollars worth of assets to the bank within a year!

Action Summary:

- ■ What objections do consumers raise about your "industry"? Provide a guarantee to solve that objection and people will flock to you.
- ■ Do you know what the number one complaint people have with plumbers? Not shoddy work, or overpricing services. It is the dirt they leave behind. One plumber realized this and made an offer: "We will clean up our mess before we leave – or you

don't pay a dime." As you can guess, people started calling them instead of their old plumbers when they needed some plumbing work to be done!

Moving Service Guarantee

Mary Ellen Sheets' two sons had a part-time moving business in the early 1980s. To help them attract new clients, Sheets drew two stick figures in a truck and placed an ad in the local newspaper.

The ad worked. It worked too well in fact. When her sons moved on to better things in 1985, Sheets hired 2 people to do the heavy lifting and continued the business. Business was brisk. But she found out that people in general didn't trust movers. Most movers were rough with stuff and charged on a weight basis. Sheets changed her business model – she started charging per hour instead of per pound and she started focusing on the local residential moving – while most of her competition focused on moving across longer distances.

Then Sheets did the unthinkable. She made a guarantee that she would pay for any damages to be fixed! No one had made such an outrageous guarantee before. If something broke while loading it, the movers weren't liable. The business boomed after that guarantee and Sheets had to expand quickly.

Last year, her little company "Two Men and a Truck" operated in 27 states, made 250,000 moves, and generated $150 million in revenue!

Action Summary:

■ Find out what people don't like about your industry. Ask questions. Lots of them.

- Then come up with an offer that solves that problem for people.
- And make a "risk reversal" guarantee – a guarantee that builds instant trust and takes away all of people's hesitation in doing business with you.

Parental Relief

Superquinn is a supermarket chain in Dublin, Ireland. The founder of the chain Feargal Quinn realized that parents had a hard time shopping with kids. So he spent a lot of money and created a playhouse in all of his supermarkets. He bought play equipment for kids and even hired a specialized staff of supervisors who could take care of the kids and entertain them while their parents shopped.

The results were that most parents started shopping at Superquinn instead of going to their competitors. Shoppers also spent more time in the store when kids weren't there annoying them, and ended up buying more goods. With more innovations like these, Superquinn gave an experience to shoppers that no other supermarket gave, and slowly captured a two-thirds supermarket share in Dublin!

Action Summary:

- Make it easier for people to shop at your place. Add a playhouse for kids if your target audience is parents.
- McDonald's built an empire by adding playhouses to their restaurants for 20 years.
- Remove people's annoyances and they'll spend more time at your place and end up buying more goods.
- Remember: you are not just selling your products. You are selling a whole experience!

No Waiting Policy

Whitlock ran a cellular phone store in West Virginia, offering both products and services. He sold cell phones and accessories and he offered to fix broken cell phones too. When people came in to buy a cell phone, they wouldn't have to wait. But if they came to get their cell phones fixed, they had to wait for at least 20 minutes to as much as 2-3 hours. Many people would come in and drop their cell phones to be fixed and collect them on the next day. But it would be inconvenient for them, as they would have to come back to the store again.

One day, Whitlock came up with a brilliant solution. He gave a new cell phone to people who came in to get their old cell phones fixed. People could leave their cell phones and go on running their errands or shopping and as soon as their cell phones were fixed, Whitlock would give them a call.

The brilliant thing about the idea is that people could test out the new cell phone model and could end up buying it or trading it in for their old cell phones and some money. Whitlock's cell phone fixing business increased and he satisfied more clients because of this simple idea.

Action Summary:

- Even if you don't run a cell phone store, it's a good idea to have a no waiting policy. You could give pagers to people so that they can carry on doing their errands and you can page them to come when you are ready.
- Quite a few expensive restaurants have already started giving people pagers if there is a waiting line. People can shop rather than waiting and being bored and these restaurants page them when a table opens up.

■ It's a small gesture but client satisfaction goes way up because of these pagers!

Selling Flowers in January

Hugh is a fantastic florist and runs a flower shop. Over many years, Hugh has found that January is the slowest month for him. The holiday season (Halloween, Thanksgiving, Christmas, and New Year) has all just gone and the biggest flower day (Valentine's Day) is still to come. Between these two biggies, January seems hidden.

One year, Hugh decides to test if advertising in January would help increase his sales. He analyzes all sorts of advertising media like newspapers and radio. But then he decides to buy a small road sign near his shop because it wouldn't cost him a lot. The road sign simply reads:

How mad is she?
Make up with a bouquet
– Atkinson Flowers

That one single road sign drove a ton of sales to Hugh's flower shop. Although not as good as sales during holiday seasons or special occasions, Hugh's January sales have never been better.

Action Summary:

■ It seems hard to adapt this case study for any other business except a flower shop (or a gift shop). But it's a good story of creative advertising.

■ Try to deconstruct the ad to see why it did so well. The ad amplified an emotion and gave people a (new) reason to give flowers. That's about it.

■ Provide people with new information or new reasoning, and they'll buy more from you.

Reach the Influencers

I wanna be like Mike...or Moses...or Britney...or...

Are we like sheep? Yes we are. Very often to sell to the masses you just need to sell to the people they look to for inspiration. Do you know that companies give away hundreds of thousands of dollars of merchandise just to get a star to be seen in their product? Brad Pitt wearing a specific brand of sunglasses or Usher sporting a certain brand of clothing can be a fast train to profits-ville for the company.

Now you don't have to spend thousands, nor do you have to get it in the hands of today's hottest movie star or recording artist. People get their influences from many places; you just need to reach the influencers.

Selling to a Salesman

William Clement Stone was born more than a century ago, in the year 1902 to be precise. Born in poverty, he became a billionaire because of his selling skills. He had seen it all, done it all. By the age of 16, he was making more than $100 per week selling insurance. In the 1930s when the whole of America was in a grave depression, he was prospering. He opened his own insurance company and by 1930, he had hired 1000 agents who brought him money week in and week out.

Don Alm wanted to sell an alarm system to W. Clement Stone. He knew it was really hard to get through the various gatekeepers and meet W. Clement in his own home. He had to find a way to meet W. Clement. Don observed that in all the photos of W. Clement, he had a rare cigar in his hand. So he found out where W. Clement bought his rare cigars and bought a box from there. The

next day he went to W. Clement's house and when the maid opened
the door, he said: "Hi! These are for Mr. Stone for FIVE minutes
of his time." The next thing you know: he spent more than an hour
with W. Clement. He sold him on the alarm system too. Clement
was so impressed with him that he referred his services to lots of
his friends too. With just a box of cigars, Don Alm created an opportunity that enabled him to sell his alarm systems to hundreds of
wealthy people.

Action Summary:

- ■ Find out who the leaders are; the influencers in your market.
  Try to sell to them. If you can satisfy them, they will recommend your services to loads of other people.
- ■ Find out what your clients like. Once you know what they like,
  your approach becomes a lot simpler.
- ■ A gift has opened lots of doors. A small upfront investment in a
  gift can lead to huge profits.

Starting With a Bang!

Fazoli's was one of the fastest growing Italian fast food chains
in America. They grew to over 400 restaurants in 16 short years.
Over the years, they've fine-tuned a system that makes sure that they
generate a lot of buzz before they open for business in a new town.
They make sure that they are a success even before they open up.
How do they do that?

Some time before opening, Fazoli's joins the chamber of commerce in the town. By being a member, they gain access to all the
other members. Then, Fazoli's sends a note to all the members of the

chamber of commerce, inviting them to come to Fazoli's for a free meal before it opens up to the rest of the town.

Many of these members, who are business owners and have a good standing in the community, show up for the free meal. It almost becomes like a chamber get together. Fazoli's does its best to impress these businessmen and women. They provide great food and terrific service. They create a festive mood by decorating the restaurant. As a result, the night makes a killer impression and gets the whole town talking about the new restaurant. Fazoli's becomes a hit restaurant in the new town even before they open up for business.

Action Summary:

- ■ Give away samples of your product freely to generate a buzz. Fazoli's gave away one night's worth of free food to create a buzz.
- ■ Reach the influential people of the community. Impress people who are well respected in the community, or are well respected in their field of business, and word about your products will spread.
- ■ Gather people to an event and give them a memorable day, and they'll become loyal to you.

Grass Roots Marketing
(This story has personally had an effect on my life)

In 1982, Dietrich Mateschitz drank a tonic drink in Asia and thought that such an energizing drink would sell very well in the Western world. In 1984, he created a formula for a tonic drink and launched Red Bull in his home country of Austria. But the launch was disastrous. The government gave them a lot of problems due to the high caffeine content in the energy drink.

In 1987, Red Bull somehow hustled their way out of the government bureaucracy and got permission to sell the drink. They didn't have a huge marketing budget to make a splash like other soft drink companies like Coca Cola and Pepsi usually made to launch a product. So Red Bull quietly started a grass roots marketing campaign.

They focused solely on their target audience: the young hip generation of 18-25 year olds, and then they sought to influence these people. They went where their target audience hung out: at discos and clubs. They started giving away free Red Bull cans for people to taste. They then sought the people who influenced their target audience: the DJs and the bartenders and educated them to promote "Red Bull with Vodka." All of a sudden, "Red Bull with Vodka" became the best selling drink in hundreds of discos and bars all over the world!

Red Bull didn't just stop there. They sought out ways to make these influencers passionate about Red Bull. Instead of simply stopping at keeping the well-known DJ's well stocked, they sought to create better DJ's! They opened a "Red Bull Music Academy." They would sponsor 60 DJ's from all over the world to come and gather in one location and have jam sessions for 2 whole weeks!

Red Bull Music Academy became so famous that more than 2000 DJ's apply for the sponsorship every year! By holding musical events for the people who influence their target audience, Red Bull made them passionate about their product! These influencers became die-hard fans of Red Bull and would spread the word about them on every chance they received.

As a result of such campaigns, Red Bull sells more than a billion cans of the energizing drink a year! Within 18 short years, Red

Bull has become a multi billion-dollar company with yearly sales in billions with very low cost grass roots-level marketing campaigns.

Action Summary:

- Decide who your target audience is. Then go and promote your products where your target audience hangs out. (Yeah, that was me)
- Influence the influencers. Figure out who your target audience listens to and then educate these influencers about your product.
- Make these influencers passionate about your company. Give them something besides money and they will talk about you and the experience you provided forever!
- You don't need to sponsor 60 influencers for a 2-week jamming session like Red Bull does. A simple free coffee and chat invitation goes a long way!

Rise of Jay Leno

Jay Leno is one of the most famous comedians and talk show hosts today. But he wasn't always this famous. Like other struggling comedians, Jay did a lot of grunt work too. He went to shady clubs in the middle of nowhere and performed there. He networked like crazy, shaking and baking with hundreds of people every month. But one trick he used made sure that his shows were full house – even though he wasn't famous.

What is that trick? He performed for free for cab drivers and their spouses. He would hold special shows especially for cab drivers at 2 in the morning.

As a result, whenever someone asks the cabbie "What's happening in the city?" or "What's the best thing to do at night?" the cab driver would tell them to go and see Jay Leno's comedy show.

Action Summary:

- You could copy this same tactic and give a freebie to cab drivers. Just call them for free dinner and showcase your product.
- Influence the influentials.
- Figure out who your target audience is. Then figure out who they listen to. Who do they look up to? And then go and persuade those people to refer people to you.
- Give a free sample to people who are in a position to influence your prospective audience.
- Demonstrate your work so that they feel comfortable referring you to others.

Selling Cranberry Juice

It's 1959 and Ocean Spray is in trouble. Ocean Spray is the biggest producer of cranberry sauce and in October 1959, the government announces that it has found pesticide residues in cranberry sauce. This pesticide residue is found in cranberry sauce not produced by Ocean Spray. But yet, the announcement throws a scare at the public and the sales of cranberry sauce decline.

The scare soon dies out as tainted supplies are withdrawn and strict inspection measures put in place. But sales are wiped out in November and December and, since very few people eat cranberry sauce except at Thanksgiving and Christmas, Ocean Spray loses a year's sales. Reacting to this grave situation, and taking precaution to avoid such a scenario again in the future, Ocean Spray executives decide to produce an evergreen product – which is bought and used throughout the year.

Their obvious choice is cranberry juice. After they start producing the new cranberry juice, they face another problem: convincing the public to buy it. Ocean Spray, like its competitors, General Mills and Kellogg's, tries building awareness through mass media channels such as radio and magazine ads. But sales aren't as high as expected. This is when Ocean Spray executives decide to focus on selling to a particular audience – a small group of the population that could persuade the rest of the world to buy cranberry juice.

Ocean Spray's whole strategy rides on getting the small group of people to persuade the rest of the population to try and taste the cranberry juice, and then buy it. Fortunately, they chose their small audience well.

They chose bartenders and doctors. Bartenders are always looking for new drinks to entice their customers and cranberry juice was an instant hit in the bars. To help the bartenders, Ocean Spray also starts promoting cranberry cocktail. The other small group, doctors, was given seminars and literature to educate them about how cranberries could help to cure bladder and other infections by reducing the ability of bacteria to live within the body. These 2 different sets of audiences started persuading people to give cranberry juice a try, and it caught on. Even though 40 years have passed, Ocean Spray hasn't changed its winning strategy. Still today they try to enlist bartenders and doctors to persuade the general public to buy cranberry juice. As a result, they hold 20% of the supermarket juice shelf!

Action Summary:

- If you sell a seasonal product, think of manufacturing a second "evergreen" product that can be sold yearlong.
- Enlist the connectors and the mavens to persuade the general public on your behalf. Educate a small part of the population - that can reach a lot of people - about your product. Provide them with free samples.
- Give them incentives to promote your product. It's easier and even cheaper to reach a smaller subset of the audience who can promote your products to the entire world.
- Which subset of the audience can sell your products to the world?

A Thousand Salesmen

There was a shop that sold clothes for all: men, women and kids. They were doing average: not too good, not too bad. The shop owner did all sorts of advertising in newspapers, magazines and billboards. But that didn't help a lot. The advertising barely increased the shop's sales.

One day, the shop owner goes to another city on vacation with his wife. After visiting a few tourist places, the couple hails a cab. The cab driver was talkative and started asking all sorts of questions to the couple. When he realized that the couple was vacationing in the town, he started offering suggestions on places to eat and things to see before leaving. This burned an idea in the shop owner's mind: why not get the cab drivers in his town to let people know about his shop?

As soon as the shop owner and his wife are back from their vacation, the shop owner calls his sales executive and tells him about his idea. The sales executive simply loves the idea and prepares to execute it.

The sales executive contacts 100 cab drivers and asks them to come for free breakfast to a posh restaurant. Almost all cab drivers come – just so that they could have breakfast in that posh restaurant for free! During the breakfast, the sales executive asked them if they would mention their shop to people who rode in their cabs. The sales executive doesn't offer to pay these cab drivers. While the cab drivers are leaving, he just hands them a free t-shirt and then he waits to see the response.

The response turns out to be better than they ever expected! These cab drivers started getting a lot of people to the clothes shop. Many vacationers came and bought a lot from the shop. Many local citizens came too. On calculation, the shop owner figures that at least 20% new business was generated because of these cab drivers. The only cost was 100 t-shirts and free breakfast! It was much cheaper than advertising in newspapers and magazines!

The shop owner and the sales executive soon host more free breakfast sessions for other cab drivers. Soon, they had 1000 salesmen who roamed the city referring people to the shop every day!

Action Summary:

- Get people who can reach and influence lots of people to become your secret salesmen.
- You don't even have to pay them money to refer others. Just give them a free gift. They will reciprocate by referring others to your store.
- Getting cab drivers to refer people to your store is a good idea. You could also get the hotel receptionist to refer the people who stay in that hotel to your store. The person who stands at the tourist information desk in airports and train stations would be another good resource.

Dare to be FCUKing Outrageous
"Yes, I kiss my mom with this mouth"

French Connection is a fashion chain that was battling other fashion chains in the UK. None of them stood out from the rest of the crowd. That is, until 1997, when the CEO Stephen Marks decided to try and break from the crowd and stand out. His goal was to make his company one of the most talked about brands. But how could he do this?

The idea came when they were communicating by fax with their new Hong Kong store that was opening up. They came across a fax "From FCHK to FCUK". The new brand strategy was to use the shortened FCUK as the company logo.

Mr. Marks was willing to risk insult to break from the mold. The result, while very controversial, increased the profits from £6m to over £19m. There are FCUK stores in over 20 countries and new ones opening yearly, and the company's stock price has gone from £3 to over £8.

FCUK has become a brand in and of itself away from just the clothing line. Now you can also get FCUK Him and FCUK Her Fragrances. It has opened more profit centers that wouldn't have been available or successful if the name was still French Connection.

French Connection UK stands out as a company that found new potential with a risqué name. They were willing to take risks that others may have seen as too dangerous and have reaped the rewards because of it.

The Mango Man

In the Caribbean lives a man named Gregory. He sells more fruit than anyone in the entire pack of islands and he sells it for more money! How does he do that? He only sells fresh fruit from his small trusty boat. But he does more than just sell fruit.

Gregory has one of the smallest motorboats and he painted it the color green, which can be easily seen in the blue sea. He has tied more than a dozen colorful flags of various kinds that he took from other ships. As if that wasn't enough for him to win people's attention from far away, he signals his arrival by blowing into a conch shell.

When children hear the conch shell, they start shouting: "It's the mango man!" Their parents dig into their pockets and buy the fruit from Gregory. Gregory makes it an occasion for tourists and their kids to eat fruit.

Action Summary:

- Gregory goes to his clients instead of waiting for his clients to come to him. By taking his business mobile, he sells more fruit than anyone else. How can you make your business more mobile?
- You can't sell if you don't have people's attention. Win people's attention by being colorful. Then follow up with your great service.
- Brand yourself. Gregory branded himself as the "Mango Man." This made people recognize him. People bought fruits from Gregory even after a few copycats started selling fruits in motor-boats in a similar way.

Martini On A Rock

In the heart of New York lies the famous Algonquin Hotel that underwent a massive renovation. The public spaces and guest rooms in the hotel were refurbished at a multimillion-dollar expense.

The hotel management thought of sending a normal press release to the media announcing their reopening. But then they chucked that idea out for a more outrageous plan. They came up with the most expensive drink on the planet. Their Martini on the Rock has a price tag of ten thousand dollars and takes 3 days to prepare!

What's so special about a martini that it costs ten grand? Well, it comes with a very expensive rock – a diamond at the bottom of the glass. When asked who would buy such an expensive drink, Anthony Melchiorri, the general manager says that he hopes "would-be grooms would use the costly cocktail to pop the question."

To date, no one has ordered the most expensive martini. But the outrageous offer has generated a lot of interest and garnered a lot of free ink for the hotel in newspapers all over the world. The best perk, the hotel might be included in the world record books. They couldn't have asked for a better reopening.

Action Summary:

- Use the power of outrageous pricing.
- Charge a wildly-high or an insanely low-price for one product, and that product will generate tremendous publicity for you, making it easier to sell your other products.
- Generally speaking, both extremely high pricing or extremely low pricing will generate publicity. The benefit of high pricing is that if there are any takers for the high-priced product, you'll make a huge profit.
- And the benefit for the extremely low price is that it will persuade many people to visit your store, who might go on to purchase your other products and you'll end up making a huge profit.

Joe and Mary's Night Out

It's December 25th. Joe and Mary are trying to get a hotel room for the night. They find none. Finding no other option, they have to go spend their night in a stable nearby. During the night, Mary gives birth to a son. Fast-forward 2004 years; Mary's son has left a long-lasting legacy. Billions of people follow his teachings. The son was none other than Jesus Christ. One hotel company is trying to make amends for the hotel industry not having any rooms left on Christmas Eve all those years ago, when the biblical couple – Mary and Joseph - was roaming Bethlehem hunting for a place to stay.

The hotel chain – Travelodge - is offering free lodging and boarding to any couple named Mary and Joseph at any of the 252 Travelodge hotels in the UK and Ireland on Christmas Eve. The couple just has to show ID to get a free room on one of the busiest days for the entire hotel industry. Travelodge sent a press release to the media outlets announcing that they welcomed any Mary and Joseph couple for free and the effect was amazing. They got free publicity worldwide. Newspapers from South Africa to Australia to America all wrote about Travelodge's offer. Many people all over the world have heard about Travelodge because they came up with a quirky and outrageous offer and sent a few press releases.

Action Summary:

- Make an outrageous offer. Give away something for free to qualified people. You read about how a restaurant gained free publicity by giving away free food to bald people and now Travelodge is gaining free publicity by giving away a free stay to any couple named Mary and Joseph.
- Select a group of people to reward. It could be "persons over

7.6 feet tall get free product" or "women wearing black nail polish get a discount."

- Send press releases to the media.
- Just like Travelodge tagged to Christmas holidays, you too can tag to festivals, occasions and other current affair news for added publicity.

Gimmick Marketing

The Justice Department of America considers online gambling to be illegal. They make life harder for every major media outlet that accepts ads from online casinos and gambling websites.

Most online gambling websites didn't think of fighting the big government. Instead, they were happy buying ads in smaller media outlets. But one website decided to find loopholes.

Goldenpalace.com wanted to become the biggest online gambling website. That wouldn't be possible if they just dabbled in buying ads where they could. So they decided to use the power of free publicity. Unfortunately, they didn't have any event or occasion that would end up getting them free publicity. So they decided to make up some.

Around the same time, a woman put a grilled cheese sandwich for sale on eBay.com. The grilled cheese had a mark on it that looked like Virgin Mary. The auction generated a lot of buzz and the media caught on to it. Goldenpalace.com thought that this would be a good opportunity to come into the media spotlight and so they outbid everyone. They finally spent $28,000 to buy a grilled cheese sandwich. In return for that, their name was included in the news on more than 200 radio and TV shows!

Traffic to goldenpalace.com exploded and they saw a big spike in the number of people who became members and started gambling because of their winning the grilled cheese auction. Because of their success, goldenpalace.com decided to add "bidding on weird auctions" to their marketing arsenal and made it a part of their promotional strategy.

Over the next few months, they bid on unusual items like Pope Benedict's old car and Michael Jackson's puppets. They spent close to one million dollars in buying up buzz-worthy stuff from eBay. com. In return, they received free publicity every time they won an auction! Some experts calculate the worth of their free publicity to be close to thirty million dollars!

After the end of every auction, goldenpalace.com saw a 25-38% increase to traffic to their website. Because of their tactic of leveraging buzz-worthy sales, they are now one of the three biggest online gambling sites in the world, getting more than 2.4 million visitors a month to gamble on their site!

Action Summary:

- Jump onto unusual advertising avenues. Be the first one to try a gimmick, and you'll earn a lot of free publicity in return.
- Tag yourself to a buzz-worthy event or sale.
- Keep an eye on international news, and if you see a trend early on in some other city or country, imitate it in your town to get local media writing about you.

Ma & Pa's Café Contest

In a small town is a 40-seat café called "Ma & Pa's Café." The owners of the café – Roxanna and Harry - want to sell the place. But they want more than what they would receive on the market. The market value of their café would not be over $100,000. So they do a little thinking and come up with an outrageous idea. They think of giving their café away to one lucky person! The person who wrote the best essay that started with "I would like to own Ma & Pa's café because..." would win the café as well as receive $50,000 in cash to spend as he wished! A free café giveaway? Doesn't that sound outrageous and crazy?

Oh but there was a small catch. To enter the contest, with their essays, people had to mail in $150 entrance fee too! And if Harry and Roxanna didn't receive 2000 entries by August 1st of that year, the contest would be cancelled and all the contestants would receive their entrance fees back.

If you do a little math, you'll find that Harry and Roxanna were looking at receiving a cool $150,000 more for their café than what it was actually worth – because of the contest!

Unfortunately, Harry and Roxanna didn't receive 2000 entries by August 1st, and they had to cancel the contest. But you can see how to use contests to sell a simple product for more money, can't you?

Action Summary:

- People love contests and will take a chance if the entrance fee is minimal and the payoff looks huge! You could use a similar idea, and make it work by making the entrance fee as low as $50, and increasing the number of contestants you are looking for.
- You could use contests in other forms too: have an offer that states 1 out of 5 buyers chosen randomly would get a 100% refund and you'll see that people will come and buy from you instead of going to the competition – in hopes of being one of the lucky 5.

■ Remember: just having a contest won't bring a lot of people to your shop. You'll have to promote the contest too.

Outrageous Pricing

Ostfriesland hotel is a three-star hotel in the Northern German town of Norden. Early this year, Heckworth, the owner, came up with an idea when a regular customer made a joke to him.

The regular customer had lost 35kgs (77 pounds) between her two visits to the hotel. In a joke, she told Heckworth that she should be charged less than before because she would now eat a lot less of that free breakfast, and there would be less wear and tear to the furniture.

The joke caught on Heckworth's imagination. He implemented a pricing scheme: charge people according to their weight instead of charging them by the room, 1 euro for every two kilos. A thin man weighing in at 60 kilos (132 pounds) would pay just 30 euros ($36), but a heftier individual topping the scales at 100 kilos (220 pounds) would have to cough up 50 euros ($60) for the night. Heckworth then sends a press release to the local newspaper. In it, he gives a reason for his new pricing scheme by saying, "Slim guests live longer and can therefore come more often. That is why we reward them."

The local newspaper writes about this new pricing scheme and other bigger newspapers, radio and TV stations catch the news from them. They all give a lot of free ink to Ostfriesland hotel. Today, because of this pricing stunt, Ostfriesland is the most visited hotel in Norden.

Action Summary:

■ I'm not suggesting that you scratch your current pricing model and implement this one of charging people by their weight. But you might want to do something outrageous. Because the more outrageous your idea, the more free press you'll receive.

- ■ The steps of coming up with an outrageous news-worthy story are simple: Select a group of people you want to reward. Then make a special offer to them. Then announce the offer through press releases.

Set Your Price

Marvin is a dentist. A few years back, he came up with a unique idea to promote his practice and have some fun during the holidays.

From Thanksgiving to New Year's, people could come to Marvin's office and receive a complete basic exam and teeth cleaning. They wouldn't be charged the usual rates. Instead, they could pay whatever they thought the service was worth! (Marvin did charge his normal rates for all the other services he provided though.)

Here are the results: most people paid the usual rates for basic teeth exam and cleaning. A few paid very little money. But these were usually the people who were putting off dental checkups due to financial problems. A few amazingly paid more money than the usual rates! All in all, people balanced each other out and Marvin just made a little less money than he usually would have if he charged his normal rates.

But here is the added bonus: because the idea was so unique, many more people came to Marvin during this time period. Many of his inactive patients showed up, and a high number of referrals showed up as his old patients told their friends about the unique "set-your-own-price" offer from their dentist. As a result Marvin's appointment book was jam-packed. Marvin made more money because of higher volume.

Many of the new clients who came to Marvin because of the offer also returned back again after the offer was over. All in all, the pricing tactic worked better than anyone had anticipated!

Action Summary:

- You could do the same thing. Select your most basic product and let people buy that for any price they see fit for a short period of time. This will generate a lot of buzz for you.
- If you send press releases to the media, you'll be written about in many newspapers.
- If you send postcards to your old clients, they'll be sure to come visit you and also tell their friends about you.
- You can then follow up and sell your other products to new clients later on.
- Another hidden advantage of this trick is it'll give you a good idea of what people think your product should cost. Disregard the extreme price points (as some people will pay you just $1 while a few will pay exorbitant rates) and then take out price point averages.

Warranty Shoes

Matthew Smith owns "Shoes for Crews" which makes safety work shoes that are guaranteed not to slip. Matthew sold the shoes to big companies with lots of employees through their "payroll deduction plans." Employers would deduct the cost of shoes directly from their employees' paychecks.

Matthew was finding it hard to attract a lot of employers who were willing to buy shoes from him exclusively. The company was struggling even though his shoes really cut employee slipping incidents and improved employee safety at work. Every employer wanted to improve employee safety, but amazingly, most of them were hesitating to commit to buy shoes from Shoes for Crews. Something was holding them back. So Matthew came up with a plan. Some people call that plan gutsy. Some call it insane.

What was the plan? Matthew offered a $5,000 warranty on every pair of shoes. Shoes that cost $50 now came with a $5,000 warranty – essentially a 10,000% money back guarantee!

If any employee slipped while at work wearing those shoes, Matthew would have to pay the claim for up to $5000. Soon after having made this warranty offer, sales started increasing. In no time, 9 out of the 10 biggest restaurant chains of America became Matthews's clients; but what about when employees slip? Even though the shoes are made using advanced technology that reduces slipping, a few employees do slip for various reasons while at work. When slipping occurs, Matthew pays up promptly. It makes sense to pay $15,000 to keep a client who buys shoes worth $2 million a year from him!

Action Summary:

- Employ "risk reversal" strategies by having a "more than 100% money back guarantee" that totally removes risk from buying.
- The trick to making risk reversal offers is simple: Find out what people's objections are, make a guarantee that overcomes those objections.
- For example: The objection of employers was they weren't sure if Matthew's shoes would actually reduce slipping. So Matthew came up with a $5000 warranty on $50 shoes plan.
- Don't be afraid and think that refund rates will sky-rocket

because of your policy. If your product is any good, your sales will increase by a much higher percentage than the amount of refunds you'll have to provide. (Of course, if you have a bad product, a risk reversal offer will put you out of business.)

Satisfaction Conviction Tactic

Sugarman is a direct marketing pioneer and a legend. One of the several products he has sold was a yearly subscription to a "discount product" newsletter. Sugarman went and searched for refurbished product deals. Then he wrote about such deals and sold refurbished products through a newsletter.

Sugarman knew that more people would buy if he could remove the risk in purchasing. So he made the usual risk reversal offer that other newsletter publishers make: subscribers could cancel anytime and get the money back for the newsletters they hadn't received.

When people came to know that they could get out of the newsletter subscription easily if they didn't like the newsletters, more of them started subscribing. But more of them started canceling their subscriptions after a few months too. However, the increase in subscribers took care of the increase in cancellations.

But then, Sugarman made an outrageous offer that goes beyond logic. He made a money-back guarantee that stated: if the subscribers didn't like and benefit from the newsletter for 2 years, they could request and receive all of their money back. Even for the issues they had read! Joe Sugarman calls such an outrageous guarantee a "satisfaction conviction" guarantee. No one had ever made such a guarantee before. Sugarman tested this guarantee and found that it pulled out three times better than the sales letter with a normal guarantee!

And did people take advantage of such a guarantee and ask for a refund after 23 months? Very rarely! In fact, Sugarman found that the refund rate was lower for the satisfaction conviction guarantee than the other more typical guarantee!

Action Summary:

- ■ Make an outrageous "satisfaction conviction" guarantee.
- ■ It will make people trust you and your offer, which will lead to a higher conversion rate.
- ■ And it magically decreases the rate of refund too. People logically think that no one can make such an offer if their product is not first class and so they value the products even before they buy them, decreasing the refund rate.

"On The House" Plan

It's 1957. One storeowner in London is looking for a magic bullet. His store is located on a back street and doesn't attract a lot of traffic. Many people who come there only come to look for the best prices and discount deals. Something had to be done to increase the sales despite the poor location of the store.

Well, the storeowner receives a magic bullet on a silver platter and soon overturns the fortunes of his store within 4 days. The deserted look leaves the store as queues of people start forming outside the store gates every day and all this happens because of one simple tactic the storeowner starts using.

The storeowner, instead of giving a normal receipt of purchase, starts giving a "timed" receipt of purchase to the customers that says the exact time of transaction. The next day, the customers can see a time period on a huge blackboard outside the store. If it says "2:20 to 2:50", any customer who had bought anything during that time span the previous day could ask for a complete refund. Every day, for half an hour, all the purchases are on the house. But no one knows which half an hour beforehand. The storeowner draws the time from slips in a hat each day after the store closes.

Because of this "on the house" plan, many people start taking detours to the back street to come to this store instead of going to other stores in much more convenient locations. His number of customers per day triples from 65 to 200. The storeowner gives away $140 worth of goods every day. But he can justify this cost as sales increased by an awesome two and a half times! Even though the markup decreases from 20% to 14% because of the 30-minute refunds, the 250% boost in sales volume doubles the store profits!

Action Summary:

- The storeowner tripled the customers and doubled the store profits by a simple "30-minute on the house" contest. You could borrow his idea for your business too.
- Contests are a great way to get people to your store instead of your competitor's store.

Pizzagra

Pizza is pizza, right? It's just a round dough base with tomato sauce, a bunch of toppings and cheese! And it hasn't changed much for hundreds of years, until now!

The UK supermarket chain "Iceland" has repackaged pizzas into something that sets "pulses racing and libidos leaping." Instead of having a round base, they are making pizzas on a heart-shaped base and they are adding toppings like artichoke, asparagus, ginger, chocolate and banana – which are said to possess aphrodisiac qualities. "Food has long been associated with the art of seduction so we're combining romance with one of the most widely-enjoyed foods in the UK," said Iceland's Steve Sweeney.

And their unique combination of toppings and the outrageous name "Pizzagra," taken from "Viagra," has got the media generating a lot of buzz and publicity for the supermarket chain.

Many local newspapers wrote about Iceland's new Pizzagra. They even received international publicity for free when CNN picked up the story!

Action Summary:

- It's easy to repackage your product and make it stand out from the competition. Just give it a different taste. Or associate it with something unusual (like Iceland associated pizza with romance).
- Give your product an outrageous name. Iceland created a bigger buzz because they named their product Pizzagra.
- If pizzas, which have been the same for dozens of years, can be repackaged, anything can! How can you repackage your product?

Taco Liberty Bell

The huge chain of Mexican food, Taco Bell, ran a full-page ad in the New York Times that read:

"Taco Bell Buys the Liberty Bell. In an effort to help the national debt, Taco Bell is pleased to announce that we have agreed to purchase the Liberty Bell, one of our country's most historic treasures. It will now be called the 'Taco Liberty Bell' and will still be accessible to the American public for viewing. While some may find this controversial, we hope our move will prompt other corporations to take similar action to do their part to reduce the country's debt."

The date when Taco Bell published this ad was April 1st, 1996! It was April Fools' Day! Taco Bell was obviously playing a trick on the public.

Thousands of people called the National Historic Park in Philadelphia that houses the Liberty Bell complaining about the decision to sell the bell. People were outraged! At noon on April 1, Taco Bell sent another press release that claimed that theirs was the Best Joke of the Day, and received even more publicity when Radio and TV stations narrated the story.

The joke paid off for Taco Bell big time. Their sales during the week of April 1st jumped by half a million dollars!

Action Summary:

- Can you come up with a better joke to cause a controversy and generate free publicity?
- A good place for brainstorming is this website: www.museumofhoaxes.com/

Getting Past the Gatekeepers

Ann Douglas is a non-fiction writer. As a mother of four, she has extensive experience in parenting. With all her experiences, it was natural for her to venture on to writing books for other mothers-to-be.

But she soon finds out that writing the book is the easy part. Getting the book published by a well-known publisher and then selling the books is the hard part. But once you've given birth to four kids, nothing stops you. Ann puts on her creative cap and comes up with an idea to reach the agents in big publishing houses before their gatekeepers can reject her.

She asks the local chocolate store to make a large chocolate "YES" for her. She then sends this "YES" - shaped chocolate with a note to prospective agents. The note says: "I hate to put words in your mouth but I really want you to represent my work…"

Ann also sends along her manuscript with the chocolate. Within no time, the tables turn. Instead of her calling and mailing cover letters to publishers only to get back rejection letters, Ann gets these publishing agents to call her up and ask her if they can still represent her work! Today, Ann is an author of 28 books, many of which are best sellers! She has established a very profitable consulting and speaking business because of her books.

Action Summary:

- This is one idea you should copy right off. Want to get an appointment? Simply send them a YES-shaped chocolate or pastry with a letter. Let the letter say "I hate to put words in your mouth but I really want you to____."
- How about a shoe box, asking to get a foot in the door?
- A hot sauce bottle, saying…if you think this is hot, check me out!
- A Pizza delivered with a slice missing…"Are you not hitting the FULL market with your advertising, are you missing a slice?"

Dr. Fun Climbs the Best Sellers List

Pat had an interesting hobby as a kid: collecting word games that were clever and a bit hard to solve. He was really smart as a kid, and no one was surprised when he landed an amazing job at NASA, where he had to develop rockets for space programs. But Pat got bored of his job at NASA! Imagine that – bored of space rockets!

To have some fun during his job, Pat started writing a book of his collected games. His book became an instant best seller when it was published. That was in 1976. Today, Pat has written 2 other books and has his own games column that is syndicated in many newspapers. He is very successful, and all his books make it to the best sellers list without fail.

And that's no magic. It's because of the tactics Pat uses to promote his books. Pat goes to bookstores all over the country to promote his books by holding book signings. But he doesn't wear suits to these book signings. Instead, he wears his rocket scientist costume! Some time back, he also started calling himself "Dr. Fun" because it was catchy and could be better remembered than "Pat Battaglia."

Pat believes that the main goal of holding book signings is not to sell books. Instead, it is to gain exposure. So he goes a step ahead of all other authors who hold book signings. He does something extra. Pat asks the bookstore manager (or the public relations manager if it's a huge bookstore) to give him a copy of their media list and then he sends a postcard to the entire media list letting them know that he is going to be signing books at the bookstore.

Pat would then follow the postcard up with phone calls and many media people would show up to cover the book signing – as they would think that this would be better than a normal book signing. "Dr. Fun would wear his rocket scientist costume, tell about his former NASA job, and then play some games from his books!"

While most authors sold a handful of books at these book signings, Pat did much better. He not only sold the books during the signing, but because of his postcards and phone calls to the media people, he would often receive a lot of free publicity and the free exposure he received would shoot his sales up!

Action Summary:

- Take a leaf from authors. These authors sell a lot of their books by making special appearances at bookstores and holding book signings. You could do the same for your product.
- Go to other shops and hold special "demonstration days" where you can show off your product, tackle questions, and make a few sales.
- Go to all the neighboring towns and cities. If you can, go to other neighboring states, and gradually, to other countries too.
- Send press releases or postcards to the local media letting them know about your demonstration day.
- Follow up with the media with a phone call making sure that they come and see you.
- Wear a funky costume, and use a short and easily memorable name, and you'll be easily remembered.

Maslowing and the Hierarchy of Marketing

"I just self-actualized, and it felt WONDERFUL!"

You have no doubt heard the old marketing story about the drill bits and the holes. I wish I knew whom to credit for the example. The example goes that thousands of drill bits are sold every year, but who wants a drill bit? People want the holes. So sell them on the value of a hole. I want to take that even further. Who wants holes in their walls? No one! They want holes to put screws in to either hold something together or hang up something. I say, sell them on how they will feel when they finally hang up that college degree, knowing that it is secure… just like your child's future. This is an example of what I have nicknamed Maslowing. I know that many people have heard of Maslow and his Hierarchy of Needs. It is a fantastic model for getting to the heart of human motivation. And isn't motivating people the purpose of our marketing? So this is a quick explanation of the Hierarchy of Needs and then how it can relate to marketing. Here is Maslow's Hierarchy:

Self-Transcendence (High)
Self-Actualization
Esteem
Love
Safety
Physiological (Low)

Physiological needs are the basic needs like food, shelter, air, sleep and water. Discomfort, sickness or death can occur when these needs are not met. It is located at the base of Maslow's design. Examples of marketing focused on this level would be help lines, suicide prevention, food banks, homeless shelters and other organizations focused on helping people who don't even have their basic physiological needs met.

Safety needs are important for feeling secure in a chaotic world. This is a desire for order, law, and security, knowing that things are available. Marketing to safety needs are insurance companies, alarm companies and car companies. A lot of companies who just give information about their services or goods get stuck here. It's comforting to know the pharmacy is open on Main Street. People feel safe knowing that your law office is "THERE".

Love needs are belonging needs. We want to receive and give love. This attracts us to groups, families and relationships. We desire to have our mate and our tribe. Love needs are marketed by showing belonging - advertising that focuses on family, clubs, memberships or romance. You see this in online dating advertising and the "join the family here at XYZ Automotive" commercials. It's also where many companies use the old bandwagon technique, "Everyone is doing it."

Esteem needs for both self-esteem and recognition from others come next. This level requires achievement, status, prestige and recognition. Many categories target the esteem need consumer, from cars to clothes, alcohol to home improvements. Many purchases are made to satisfy the esteem needs, so you will find lots of marketing here.

Self-Actualization is the need to become more than what you are. Here you seek peace, knowledge and self-fulfillment. Many colleges and universities market towards people in this area of the Hierarchy. Most people don't reach this category so many advertisers don't target them.

Self-transcendence occurs when you help others achieve their potential. Being a level farther than a level that most people do not ever reach, this is a hard area to target. What do you sell to a person who has everything that they will ever need in life and only wants to help others reach self-actualization? This is such a small target audience; dollars would be better spent in other areas.

Maslow's theory in a nutshell is that the basic needs of a human must be met before the other needs become motivating factors. The general needs, starting from the bottom up, of physiological, safety, love and esteem must be met for a person to grow up the Hierarchy. For example, someone who doesn't have shelter, food and water, doesn't worry so much about self-esteem needs, for they are higher on Maslow's Hierarchy of Needs. Once levels are achieved, higher needs become dominant, and when these in turn are satisfied, again a new and higher need emerges, and so on.

People are on all different levels of the Hierarchy. Just because someone meets a higher level, like love, doesn't mean that they quit worrying about safety; it just becomes less of a concern, thus less of a motivating factor. Many of these needs overlap, such as people who haven't really found a tribe but will use esteem needs to try and attract one. There is great value in looking at where your current marketing effort is focused.

Saving the Memories

Memories Scrapbook Store ran a successful scrapbook store that offered classes as well as a wide line of products that delighted all levels of scrapbookers. (Is that a word?) They had thousands of different paper designs, stickers, die cuts and the largest selection of all things scrapbooking clients loved. This is exactly what their advertising campaign showed. Long shots of the store were accompanied by lists of products and a class schedule.

They were looking for more return on their marketing investment. If they approached it by looking at why someone would want to scrapbook, they might find a stronger story to tell. The new campaign showed a grandmother sitting with her granddaughter. They were going through the grandma's scrapbook looking at pictures.

The commercial touched on the fact that the little girl's mother was a cheerleader too.

Would it be more motivating if they reminded the consumer that they don't want to lose those memories, or they want to have something to share with their grandchild? Prior to this plan, the company spent large amounts of ad dollars to tell the customer that you would find exactly what you would expect to find at a scrap-booking store, but never why you would want it.

Action Summary:

- ■ How many of your campaigns involve telling people what they already know about your company?
- ■ Informative commercials are on the safety level. Can you step back to why people would want your product and promote this?
- ■ Changing the level of marketing can bring more people to the table who want your product instead of fighting for those who already want your service.

What's Riding on Your Tires?

Many tire advertisements will tell you about the quality of their tire, how they grip the road and won't let your car roll over. This is a basic "safety need." Then along come Michelin tires. They let you know that your tires are safe, but why? Because in a move towards a higher need level, they provide safety for your babies.

"Because so much is riding on your tires," the visual is a little diapered baby sitting in a Michelin.

They went beyond the safety level and incorporated the love

level as a motivating factor. Basic advertising rules would have been to talk about what tires do, and discuss how well they do it. You have heard them all: Thick walls, road resistant, hug the turns, last a long time. Michelin asked "Why was all that important?"

Action Summary:

- Ask "Why is our product or service important?
- Can this be taken to a higher level on Maslow's Hierarchy?
- Has someone already claimed this position?
- What will I lose if I change levels?

Packaging to Be Different
I believe mine is bigger than yours!

In a world with so many choices, why be like everyone else? You won't always get chosen just because people take notice, but you will be on the table as an option when people recognize you. Since forced human motivation isn't available in the marketing world, and is illegal in most countries, getting on the table as an option sounds like a pretty good place to be.

The Pantyhose Revolution

The 1970s are known as the decade of revolution. Neil Armstrong has just jumped on the moon. The first test tube baby is born. Intel introduces a microprocessor that revolutionizes the computer industry. There is advancement on the civil rights front. The Beatles break up, Elvis dies. Everything is undergoing change. So it came as no surprise when the women's hosiery market underwent a revolution too.

For many years, the women's hosiery market remained stagnant and showed no signs of growing. That all changed in 1970 when L'eggs Pantyhose enters the market. Since the very beginning, L'eggs decides to separate themselves from the pack and create a radical product difference. L'eggs decides to do everything opposite. While every brand of hose comes in flat, two-dimensional packages in the shape of a leg, L'eggs pantyhose is crumpled up in a ball and comes in 3D plastic eggs. The packaging isn't only different, but also easily recognizable in the stores.

While all other brands of hosiery are sold in department and specialty stores, L'eggs sets up displays in grocery and drug stores and calls it "L'eggs Boutiques." They revolutionize the distribution system too. To attract attention, L'eggs buys its own fleet of trucks that pull up in front of each store. Then a female driver, wearing the L'eggs product and tight pants, delivers L'eggs products through the front door of the stores instead of the back door.

The buzz is enormous. L'eggs does such a good job of differentiating itself from the competition that it becomes the best-selling hosiery brand in the country within a year of its introduction!

Action Summary:

- When you are new in the market, you can win a lot of attention by doing things completely opposite than the leading company. When the competition zigs, you zag!
- Completely overhaul the packaging of your products. L'eggs doesn't change the product one bit, just the packaging. Yet it captures a lot of market share.
- Sell where others aren't selling. List all the places where your product can be bought or consumed. Then start selling there. Create your own, completely new selling booths. Coca-Cola introduced vending machines. L'eggs introduced "L'eggs boutiques." In which new places can you introduce your product?
- Win attention from your distribution system. Stick your logos and phone numbers on the cars you drive, on the company vans. Even on the t-shirts you wear.

Repackaging the Low-carb Book

The book "South Beach Diet" became an instant hit as soon as it was published. It is a slightly modified version of the Atkins diet and soon after Rodale had published it, it started climbing the bestseller lists. When Waterfront Media published the ebook version of South Beach Diet at southbeachdiet.com, they thought it would be a massive hit online too.

But unfortunately that wasn't so. The ebook version didn't catch on. Bo Peabody, the founder of Waterfront Media, who had earlier sold Tripod.com to Lycos.com, was quoted as saying: "A book is incredibly compelling in the hands of a reader on the beach, but not so compelling when it's in digital form on the computer screen." Was this the end of the ebook fad?

Fortunately, Bo Peabody didn't give up. He asked an important question: how could he make an ebook compelling on computer screens? He found a solution that solved his problems: Make the ebook interactive. To complement the ebook, he added a few interactive features such as a shopping list generator, a meal planner and a message board. He also started a beach buddies service to pair carb-conscious eaters who share similar weight-loss goals.

They weren't selling a book online anymore. They were selling a whole new package! They increased the price of the whole package too and made millions!

Action Summary:

- ■ What works offline might not work online. But by repackaging the offline product for online use, you can bring in even better results.
- ■ Add more value to your products by providing interactive features and then you can easily increase prices earning more money.

The Power of Free P.R.

Yes, jump monkey boy, jump!

Since making a salient message takes time, dedication and energy, and repetition costs money, it would seem to make sense to take advantage of public relations. A good P.R. campaign can bring you millions in publicity that you couldn't have purchased. There is much more to P.R. than sending press release after press release and hoping that someone gives a dang. It takes time, dedication, energy and repetition…or some great case studies to pilfer from.

Picket Marketing

Gerald was a hypnotist. His office was located on the second floor of a building located on a heavily-traveled highway. He was a good hypnotist. But he wasn't well known. He wanted to change that.

This is what he did: He paid a few aged people who had nothing better to do than play cards the whole day to make some picket signs and protest against hypnotism in front of his building.

A week later, the picket signs were made. The mass of elderly people came and stood waiting under the building very early in the morning. They started shouting slogans and waved their picket signs that said:

- *"Hypnotism is the work of the devil"*
- *"Hypnotism is evil"*
- *"Hypnotism is mind control"*
- *"Save our children"*

As soon as the rally started, Gerald went to his office and started placing calls to the local newspapers and television stations.

Within half an hour, newspapers and television stations sent over their reporters and photographers. The TV stations featured the news story on the 9 o'clock news. He also made it to his local newspaper and his photo was published too. All of a sudden, he became an instant celebrity in the neighborhood. His business increased.

Action Summary:

- Controversy has the potential to bring in loads of free publicity for your business.
- It's easy to create a controversy. You don't necessarily have to pay someone to come and start a rally. You just need to have a strong opinion and speak out about that opinion.
- But be careful - many people have been burnt before.
- Public opinion can sway either way and if it sways against you, you will be in deep trouble.

Leveraging the Elections

Becky owns an upscale steakhouse. About 2 months before the 2004 US presidential elections, Becky starts a contest at her restaurant that generates some free publicity for her. All diners are given a choice of 2 ketchups they can use with their meals: The Heinz or the W ketchup.

John Kerry's wife, Teresa Heinz Kerry, is the heiress of the company that makes Heinz ketchup. W ketchup is made by a Republican supporter, who didn't want to eat the Heinz ketchup and support the Democrats.

Becky gives each diner an opportunity to cast a vote in favor of the ketchup they like. She says: "As patrons are paying for their meals, they are handed a jellybean and asked to put it in a jar favoring Heinz ketchup or the jar indicating W ketchup."

In September, she sends press releases to media outlets letting them know about her unofficial poll and receives plenty of free publicity.

Then on Nov. 1, Becky tallies the votes and sends one more press release to the same media outlets letting them know about the winner of her polls. This time, she receives even more publicity as it's just one day before the elections.

Alas! Her polls didn't accurately predict the elections. Her diners overwhelmingly select Heinz over W ketchup and George W ends up winning the elections. Even though her polls are poor predictors, Becky is richer because of it!

Action Summary:

- ■ Piggyback on current affairs. Read the news. Then associate your product with the news. Send press releases and you might receive some media publicity for free.

President on a Parachute

The Parachute Industry Association (PIA) holds an international symposium every year. In 1997, Dan Poynter was the president of PIA and he wanted to make the symposium into a huge success. He wanted to put PIA on the map and make people aware of parachuting as a sport and fun event. The problem was PIA didn't have a lot of money to advertise on a national scale.

So Dan hired Linda Credeur, a publicist, to get the PIA symposium into the news. Linda started contacting media personnel and started pitching the symposium. The response was lukewarm. Hundreds of events were held every day, and if lucky, PIA would just manage to get ink on the 8th page of the newspaper.

To make media go crazy after you, you need to do something extraordinary, something different. Linda was fervently looking for that extraordinary hook that could make the symposium into a media-worthy event and luck favored Linda. Linda heard that George Bush Sr. is the only American president to ever parachute. As soon as Linda heard that, she started putting things into motion.

The fact that George Bush charges tens of thousands of dollars to make an appearance didn't stop her. Linda contacted everyone and asked if they knew anyone who knew George Bush. She extended her net far and wide and within a day or two, she found someone who knew Bush. Linda immediately made initial contact and invited George Bush to come to the convention. She then offered to honor George Bush and give him an award.

And what do you know? The only time George Bush had parachuted was during World War 2, and in adverse conditions. George Bush wanted to bring closure to that event. So he agreed to parachute again. As part of a carefully-orchestrated P.R. stunt, the 73-year-old former president of America parachuted during the PIA symposium. The media went bananas! They talked about the event for seven whole days and put an otherwise mediocre convention on the map. Public interest in parachuting after the event went sky high!

Action Summary:

- There are many such hidden stories that you can leverage to win free publicity. Ask yourself: is there anything special in how you make your product? In how you sell your product? Do you have any famous clients? Can you relate your industry to history?

- ■ Ask questions, dig a bit, and you'll find a great story that the media will love.

- ■ Start networking. Build a contact list so that, during crunch time, like Linda, even you can extend your network and ask all your contacts if they know someone who knows someone who knows the President.

- ■ Hold an event. Honor extraordinary people in your field. Holding events is a great way to bring all your clients together and make them more loyal and it's media-worthy too.

Making a Difference by Not Making a Dime

Monica, a young hairstylist in Waco, TX, was new to the community and needed to make a splash in order to grow business. Around the city was a large push for Breast Cancer Awareness. Her mother was a survivor of breast cancer and this was a cause very close to her heart. The campaign that she launched was called "Making a Difference by Not Making a Dime." She would donate 100% of everything she made for the month of September to cancer research. She prepared a bit in advance to be able to make a claim this bold.

When this was sent out as a press release to the media, the CBS affiliate did a news story on her, the ABC affiliate brought her in for a noon newscast interview and countless bloggers and radio mentions were made. Easily a few thousand dollars in P.R. was received but that wasn't all.

Ted Nugent (Yes…That Ted Nugent!) and his wife Shemane, after hearing of Monica's pledge, offered to match her donation. This brought even more promotion. Ted and his wife are huge supporters of this cause. Ted (Yes…That Ted!) put a large pink ribbon on his next album "Love Grenade" in support for Breast Cancer Awareness. (Yes…That Ted Nugent!)

Monica got a lot of promotion and made a sizeable donation to a non-profit and at the end of the day, could feel good about what she did to earn it.

Action Summary:

- Find a cause that is close to your heart
- Are you in the position that you could donate 100% to a cause? A number like that gets attention, much more than 10% or 15%.
- Never underestimate the power of a news story for gaining attention.
- As a new stylist, she wasn't making much money…a stronger competitor couldn't match the offer because it would probably be too much money.
- This is the kind of promotion that just feels good because you get to make a difference. Customers don't just choose you based on what you say, they watch what you do.
- Yes…That Ted Nugent! Pick up Love Grenade.

Tagging to Movies

"It's Just Lunch" is an old school dating service. Unlike other computer-based dating services where one can find their dates through a search engine, It's Just Lunch interviews a person and then manually matches them with another who has a compatible personality. Then they hook the two people up for a lunch date. They claim their services to be a stress-free way of finding potential partners. But because of their personalized services, their rates are high too. Not many people who hear about them hire them. So It's Just Lunch has to play the numbers game. Attract more people, and at least a few of them will become paid clients!

To spread the word about their services, It's Just Lunch uses a unique marketing idea. They tag themselves to recent movies to receive free publicity.

In February, just before Valentine's Day, they interviewed 3810 singles and asked them what they thought the best date movie was. They collected and compiled the answers (top movie was *The Aviator* starring Leonardo DiCaprio) and sent a press release to the media. The media jumped on the statistics and promoted It's Just Lunch for free – ahead of all the other dating services that sent a normal press release talking about their services!

Recently, just before the release of The Wedding Crashers (a movie about two guys crashing weddings to meet girls), they took another survey. This time, they asked 2774 singles if they found romance at weddings and compiled the answers and sent it to the media again. The media didn't disappoint them and It's Just Lunch received even more publicity for free! (By the way, only 3% of respondents said they had met someone at a wedding!)

Action Summary:

- ■ Tag your product or your company to the current affairs to receive free publicity. Tag it to movies, or to politics, or local news, or weather. Media is always looking for stories related to the new hot news. Provide them the stories and they will promote you for free.

- ■ Take surveys on current news and then compile the answers and send them to the media. (Make sure you somehow relate your company to the survey topic, and then enjoy the free publicity ride!)

Packaging PR

Cliff is a marketing and public relations man. He promotes his clients by using low-cost marketing ideas. His favorite tool of the trade is PR. It's more believable, doesn't take a lot of time, and best of all – it's free!

Cliff doesn't send press releases to the media on every small news event, though. He waits for the right newsworthy event, and creates one for the company if necessary. He knows that if he sends press releases without much value to the reporters, they will form a habit of ignoring his future press releases.

One tough client Cliff receives is a new lawn furniture maker. Cliff knows that a new line of a boring product like lawn furniture won't make for exciting news. So he learns all he can about the company and finds out that they make all their furniture from recycled milk carton plastic. This is better news and might win a few blurbs for Cliff in the back pages of a few smaller newspapers. But how could he make the news even more exciting?

Cliff gets a very creative idea. He packages the press releases into plastic milk cartons – the ones that are used to make the furniture. Then he mails these milk cartons to the media.

Sending press releases this way was a bit more expensive than simply faxing them. But the added expense is worth every penny. Cliff earns very valuable press time for his client in many of the bigger newspapers and other media outlets worth thousands of dollars!

Action Summary:

- The first rule of marketing is: win people's attention. The first rule of press releases is: win reporters' attention. Most PR pros win attention by using great headlines. But if you think outside of these headlines, you'll do much better.

- Take caution, though. If you send a small gift or a product sample along with the press release, many reporters and news outlets will consider it a bribe – and they won't write about you. Thus your best bet lies in the packaging of the press releases. Be creative in the "envelopes" you use to send the press releases. Don't make them too expensive (don't send a TV with a video in it). But make them different and noticeable (in a good way).

Go to Where the Customers Are!

Father of marketing technique…and convicted felon, Willy Sutton

You might remember Willy Sutton. He was a smart man. But he used his intelligence in a wrong way and for the wrong reasons. He looted banks. He was wanted for robberies in Miami, New Orleans and New York. He was so ingenious in his robberies that people spoke about him in reverent tones.

His methods were respected in a fearful way, until he was caught on March 9, 1950. After he was caught, a reporter asked him: "Why did you plunder banks?" Without blinking, he replied: "Because that's where the money is."

Willy did the wrong deeds. But he got one thing right: Go where the money is. Target an audience who has money and who is willing to spend it.

Burger King implemented this basic idea in their marketing strategy. What was their strategy? Open up stores in close proximity to McDonald's. They targeted a location where people who like eating at fast food joints already go and to attract these people to come eat at Burger King instead of McDonald's, they started customizing the meals. They custom made burgers when others were mass producing them.

Within each organization there are levels or barriers that must be crossed to make business happen. It could be putting the order in, getting samples, signing multiple copies or getting commercials created. One of the things you can do to help business grow is make it easy to do business with you. The first major obstacle is getting the customer to come to you. You can overcome this problem by going to where the customers are, and thank you, Willy, for the sage advice.

The Hypno-bus

Gerald, the hypnotist, had a student who became famous due to his antics. His student didn't want to wait long to build credibility. He wanted instant fame and fortune and so he bought a 25-foot-long motor home with a rear entrance. He completely gutted out the kitchen, tables and chairs from the motor home. Then he decked out the whole motor home. He soundproofed the walls, re-paneled and re-carpeted the interiors. He installed 4 comfy chairs. He created the first hypno-bus!

He painted the outside of the motor home with big dark words: Mobile Hypnosis Office. He started his hypnosis practice. He became wildly successful and attracted hundreds of clients.

- Some days, he would park the hypno-bus in front of a gym or exercising center and place a board out that said "Mobile office for motivation to exercise and control weight."
- Other days, he used to park at a golf course tournament and place a huge sign: "Lower your scores with hypnosis."
- He would change his location every other day and attract new clients.

Because he did something that no one else had done before, he got loads of free publicity in the local media. He became famous.

Action Summary:

- You can instantly increase your client base if you can take your business mobile. Make it easy for people to access your services and they will choose you over your competition. They will come to you even when you charge more.
- Gerald's student went where there was a demand for his services. Soon he had more clients than he needed. Go where there

is a demand instead of advertising to create a demand.

■ The student adapted with the people's wants. Adapt your services to what people want and you will earn more business.

■ Do something outrageous and different and the media will be sure to give you some free publicity.

Renting More Videos

Shane and Clarice started a video rental store. But they soon found out that it is hard competing against big video rental chains like Blockbuster and Hollywood Video, and a website that offered video rental services - Netflix.com - was making things even harder for them. Shane and Clarice knew something had to be done, and quickly. They rather liked the Netflix.com business model, which allowed people to rent 2 movies at a time, and pay $20 a month without being charged late fees. Netflix.com would send people a new movie of their choice when they returned an old one through mail...people didn't have to leave their homes to rent the videos.

Shane and Clarice didn't have enough money to compete against Netflix.com. So they decided to adapt the Netflix.com model for their own neighborhood. They decided to focus on the group of people whose chance of being Netflix.com subscribers was low. They went for the senior citizens who didn't have access to computers.

While Netflix.com uses postal mail to send and collect videos, Shane and Clarice decided to provide personal home delivery of the rental videos to the senior citizens. The couple canvassed buildings where more senior citizens lived, and got them to sign up for a service, whereby they would receive 4 videos a week for $19.99 a month. They chose buildings that were near each other, so that it would be convenient for them to go there - once each week to collect the old movies and rent new movies.

Senior citizens were grateful for their service, as it meant that they didn't have to go to video rental stores themselves. Soon, they started telling their neighbors about the video rental service. More people from the same building would signup. It wasn't unusual for Shane and Clarice to have 25% of the residents of a building as their subscribers.

By focusing on the target audience that others were ignoring, and providing better accessibility and more convenience to their clients, Shane and Clarice not only survived, but also thrived among their competition.

Action Summary:

- Make your products and services more accessible to your clients. Provide home delivery. Make house calls. Take your business mobile. You'll get more clients, many of whom will pay you more for their comfort too.
- Select and focus on a target audience that your competitors are ignoring. It's better to be the big fish in a small pond, than to be a small fish among whales in a larger pond.

"Stuff Happens"

Mark Twain once said, "A bank is an institution that lends you an umbrella when the sun is shining, but wants it back the minute it begins to rain." Banks have a bad reputation. They are seen as money-hungry institutions that do anything to increase profits. Bank of America tried to change that opinion.

Bank of America found that when a person opens an account in a bank while he is young, if he is provided satisfactory services, he will stick with the same bank until he dies. So they started focusing on getting college students to choose them as their bankers, and providing great service to these students.

- They built joint ventures with major universities all over America and would have a bank orientation program when the semester started.
- They tried to convince the parents to open a bank account for their children with Bank of America.

But they had problems implementing the second tactic of providing satisfactory services. Due to inexperience, many youngsters would make mistakes and incur different fees. This caused great disappointment. So Bank of America came out with a "Stuff Happens" card.

Now when a youngster made a mistake for the first time, for example if he would run into overdraft fees, he could use his "Stuff Happens" card and waive the fees. To redeem the card, he had to go to the bank and meet with an associate who would educate the young client about the activity that drove the mistake.

This small tactic of waiving the fees for the first mistake made Bank of America a favorite among students.

Action Summary:

- Targeting. Target an audience that will bring you the largest profits over a lifetime.
- Loyalty. Build loyalty by providing great service. Forgo a small profit now if that satisfies your clients. They will come back to do more business with you once they are satisfied and then you will have a chance of making bigger profits.
- Education. Educate your clients and they will stick with you for a long time.

Killer Auto-Service Strategy

Dan Domerofski works for many years in a company as a financial analyst. But one day, he is fired. He searches for another replacement job for weeks, but with no luck. Frustrated, he decides to be his own boss and open his own business. But his new business idea confuses many. It's nothing remotely related to finance and spread sheets. Out of the blue, Dan decides to launch an auto-service business.

He buys the equipment and announces to the world that his "EQ-oil Changes" is open for business. But the start is slow. He doesn't get many customers. That will all change when Dan changes his marketing strategy.

Instead of waiting for customers to come to him, Dan decides to go to his customers. But he realizes that it wouldn't be worthwhile to knock on every door. So he decides to knock on only "big" doors - only on doors that lead to many clients at once.

Dan starts going to office complexes and knocking on the doors of big companies. He starts offering on-worksite automotive oil and filter changing services to employees of companies only. Soon, employees of about a dozen companies of the locality rely on him to service their cars while they are busy working in their cubicles and offices. Today, Dan earns more servicing automobiles than he did in his job as a financial analyst.

In a recent interview with USA Today, Dan said: "It's been easy getting business. The secret is to come up with a chore that the average employee doesn't have time to do during the week, and find a way to do it for him while he is at work."

Action Summary:

- As Willy Sutton says: go where the money is. Instead of going to individual car owners' homes, Dan went to office complexes where many car owners are found together.
- Target a place where many of your prospective clients can be found together.
- Dan made his service more accessible than the other oil changing shops.
- One of the easiest ways to blow away your competition is to make your product or service more accessible to people.
- Make it easy for them to do business with you and your sales will increase.

Getting the Message Out

You may have noticed that in the book, we didn't really go too deep into any specific media choices. It doesn't discuss using Radio instead of T.V. or Internet over Newspaper. When it was mentioned, it was in the theme of telling how the story actually transpired. If the client used direct mail, radio or television, we just relayed the story. There is a reason for this. At the end of the day, the strategy outweighs the method of delivery. A good strategic plan with a weak budget can actually perform better than a well funded plan that has no strategy.

There are advantages and disadvantages to each method of delivery. Realize that I will be doing media outlets a big disservice putting them all into one chapter. To write about the strengths, weaknesses and how to use the different methods of delivery, with examples of clients who have done it, could fill another book... (hmmm??!? Could that be foreshadowing?) But now that we are close to the end of the book, hopefully you have seen an idea or two that you think could be applied to your business. Now how do you get the word out?

The methods of delivery can be broken down into Active, Passive and Permissive. Active media is the method through which, looking at it or not, the message is placed in front of you. Active media tend to hit you while you are doing something else and they actively get in your head. These tend to be your broadcast advertising channels such as radio, television, cable and internet pop up ads. Passive media is where the information is there, but the customer has to choose to take the information in. They have to choose to read the article, advertisement or click the link. These tend to be newspaper, magazine, internet articles and billboards (although billboards can almost be considered active). Permissive Advertising has been around but has taken off over the last few years with the increase of social media channels. It is called permissive because it has a touch of Active advertising to it in the fact that the information can be sent directly to your screen or inbox without you choosing to receive the advert. It's a bit passive in that when the info comes to you, you are required to take the next step to increase the value of the information from the business, and it's permissive in the fact that you can sign up to receive the information from the companies that you want to know about. There is a lot of value to having clients request a relationship with your company because they are obviously interested in your product or service so there is a higher chance they will do business with you when they are in need of what you sell. Permissive media is also known as "Social Media". This includes your MySpace, Facebook, Twitter, Newsletters, Blogs, Mail Lists and Email Lists that people sign up for.

Each form of advertising has strengths and weaknesses but I am a fan of advertising in general. With the power of the internet and the usage levels as high as they are, it makes sense to not only use your active and passive media to inform and introduce but to encourage the relationship to become deeper through permissive media.

The active media are great ways to introduce an idea that is new, a product or service that you want more people to know about. It's a great way to bring customers to the table. They are the easiest ways to build a brand around your company. You can use active advertising to gain customers and to invite them to join into a relationship with permissive media. You can bring new customers to your industry as well as your company.

There are challenges with active media. The price is usually a substantial investment to get enough frequency to be effective. Very often, clients spread their budgets too thin to try and be on multiple channels or stations. If your budget isn't stretching to get a good frequency on multiple outlets, minimize the number of channels or stations and focus on fewer places. There are other things affecting the active world of advertising. Scan buttons, IPods, and Satellite Radio have certainly weakened the effectiveness of radio, DVR and Internet Video have done the same thing to cable and broadcast television. There was a time when you could buy a commercial in the three "Nightly News" programs on the major affiliates in a town or place an ad in the top three radio stations morning drives and almost everyone in town would have heard about you. Due to all the options available with stations, channels and websites, audience splintering has weakened the effectiveness overall. However, even with these challenges to the effectiveness, they are still the most powerful way to hit many people with a strong frequency. This only means that the need for a strong strategy and salient message is even more important now than before. To get the word out about your strategy, I am a huge fan of active media.

Passive media's strength is in its ability to pack large amounts of information into its adverts. With some of the magazine or web articles, you can target pretty tightly into specific areas including people who are interested in your company. Again, if they are interested in your product it makes sense to do what you can to invite them to a permissive medium.

The challenges to passive media are similar to those in active media in that the price usually requires a substantial investment. Many newspapers have taken some incredible losses over the last few years and the readership of the paper version has fallen substantially. They are facing similar challenges with multiple options as well. The online competition for readers is endless. Investing in a proper website and keeping it up to date are no longer options, but necessities, as even the yellow pages are being replaced with the internet. Passive media is a great support for a well planned strategy, but without a strategy, it's weaker today than ever.

Permissive or Social Media's biggest advantage is that it has little or no cost, other than your time. It will not reach as many people as active media, but the smaller number of people usually has a high value because they are interested in knowing about your product or are already customer or fans of your company. Once a potential customer has accepted a relationship with your social media marketing platform, it is important that you keep information about your products, services, schedules, launches or events updated regularly. To keep it effective, you need to read the policies and make sure to develop a business page, as opposed to trying to run a business off a personal page. Some of the social media companies have rules about these. You need to keep your tweets or status updates common (as you stay high on the lists) and they must support your strategy. Again, if I haven't shown you thus far, I will say it again.

All of these methods can be effective, but you need to have a plan as to what you are doing and why you are doing it. You can twitt all day long about how beautiful the day is, what you're doing or your favorite Dane Cook quote, but that doesn't necessarily move your brand or company forward. Some companies tend to reward their "friends" with discounts, special shopping hours or VIP events. Your social media platform needs to align with your company strategy and support it at every level. Give the people who accepted your relationship some value for having accepted it. Take a hint from the "Golden Girls" and "thank them for being a friend" (I'm going to be humming that song all day now).

As a fan of advertising I never want to convince someone that any form doesn't work, because they all do. They just work in different ways and according to how much you have available to spend, they will have different levels of effectiveness. Putting a good strategic plan into action, however, will increase the effectiveness hands down, regardless of how you plan to promote it.

Direct Mail Case Studies
Make me pretty so they will want to look at me

Direct mail is a good tool for advertisers. It gives you the chance to target directly to zip codes or towns. If your direct mail has a response rate of 1-2% it's a home run. It always was frustrating because if you performed your job at a 1-2% success rate, you'd probably be fired, but we accept it from direct mail.

One of the most successful direct mail campaigns is the Publishers Clearing House (pch.com). They increased their response rate phenomenally by pushing customers to recognize their mail out with television. Synergy is one way to create a stronger direct mail response rate.

Magazines also found a way to create a stronger response rate with their subscription cards. Have you ever noticed that some of them are attached to the magazine and others are just loosely lying in between pages? They found that when the card falls out of the magazine, the consumer bends over to pick it up and for that brief 3- second period focuses on their card. The moment of focus caused there to be a spike in response from the cards.

So one tip about direct mail is this: figure out how to get someone to pay attention to it, either by telling them to "Watch your mailbox for our letter" or by making them look at it as they pick it up off the ground. You can also do like Mike Stepto's Bar-B-Q Shack and put an incredible and true offer on the front.

By putting direct mail into your advertising mix you can see some incredible results. You should study and practice the mail piece to increase your results, realizing that making direct mail response increase from 1-2% to 3-4% return means that the profits are doubled, thus making direct mail an incredible tool to learn how to use.

Free Earring Through the Mail

A jewelry shop owner was doing good business and earning $150,000 a year in net profits. Most of his business happened because of the amazing location of his shop.

The jeweler wanted to generate even more business and decided to use direct mail. He chose a mailing list that consisted of people staying in posh residential areas, and earning $50,000 a year or more. These were the people who would be most willing to buy from his shop. The jeweler also paid a bit more, and got names that only consisted of people who had bought something because of a direct mail letter sent to them in the past.

He sent a simple letter to these people. The letter consisted of a card and earrings...rather just one earring. The card said that if the person would come to the jewelry shop and buy anything worth $50 or more from there, they would receive the other earring for free.

The number of people who came to the jewelry shop to buy something increased a lot due to the direct mail campaign. The jeweler found that people saved the single earring and the card for months (one woman saved it for 9 months), and when they were ready to shop for jewelry, they would come to his shop, instead of going to one of his competitors' shops. Many people drove as much as 30 miles to come to his shop! As a result of this direct mail campaign, the jeweler quadrupled his net profits to $600,000 in one year!

Action Summary:

- One of the most important factors in a successful direct mail campaign is the quality of the list. If you target people who have higher incomes, and who have previously bought because of direct mail, your chances of the campaign being successful will increase dramatically.

■ Select an audience that is willing as well as able to buy your products.

■ If your product can be broken down into two, send one half of it to people for free and sell the second part.

■ Provide a free goodie to people if they spend more than a certain dollar amount at your store. This will get them to shop at your store instead of going to your competitor.

Power of Personalization

International School of Management (ISM) in Dortmund, Germany conducted marketing research to test and track the difference in results obtained by "personalizing" offers. They convinced the Municipal Utility in Dusseldorf, Germany to allow them to run a few tests on their new offer. The Utility had just started offering a price advantage to people if they signed up for a 1-year contract. ISM decided to test the offer by sending direct mail to 1400 prospects. They divided the 1400 prospects randomly into 2 groups with each group having 700 people in it.

Group A was sent an envelope that contained a general brochure that showed the cost benefits of the new offer. The prospects could use the order page at the end of the brochure to sign up for the yearly contract.

Group B was sent an envelope that contained a very similar brochure. There was only one difference: the brochures were personalized and incorporated those prospects' power usage statistics and their expected cost savings if they signed up for the yearly contract now. ISM then simply waited for the responses to come in through mail. They tracked the responses for the duration of 7 weeks. They had expected Group B to perform better than Group A. And the test showed that their expectations were accurate. But even they were surprised by the terrific response. Thirty eight of the 700 prospects from Group A signed up. That was a 5.4% response rate, which is pretty good. And 106 of the 700 prospects from Group B signed up! That is an awesome 15.1% response rate – almost three times the response of Group A!

Even though personalizing brochures cost a few cents more per mail, they more than made up for the extra printing expense by pulling in an awesome 2.8 times better response.

Action Summary:

■ If personalization on paper can boost response by 280%, imagine what it can do if used face-to-face!

■ Start collecting information about your best prospects, and send them personalized offers. Show them the exact benefits they can expect to derive from your products. Even though this will cost some time and money, the higher response rate will more than make up for any inconvenience.

■ Waiters have doubled their tips by calling the payer by name while presenting the bill. Imagine how much more you can make by just personalizing your offers.

The New Target Audience

Max Grassfield owns a men's clothing store in Denver, Colorado. He used to classify his clients into two lists:

    1. *The active clients (who bought often)*

2. *The not-so-active clients*

Max would then send offers and reminders to his clients through the mail many times a year. He would mail his active clients more often than the non-active clients, as they were more responsive and profitable. He also rewarded his active clients with gift certificates from time to time. Some time back, Max added another category to classify his clients into: The wives!

He started collecting the names of wives of people who shopped at his store. And in September, Max sent a letter to the wives. He personalized these letters by using the wives' actual names. And he referred to their husbands by name in the same letter too. With the letter, Max enclosed a $20 gift certificate that these wives could use to buy a gift for their husbands for the holiday season. Max followed this letter up with a postcard reminder in October.

The results were staggering! Max had mailed out 3,115 letters. Out of that, 154 wives came to Max's store and used the $20 gift certificate. That did cost Max some money. But the average sale was $392 per wife! In all, the whole campaign generated $60,368 in sales and increased Max's November revenue by 25% over last November!

Action Summary:

- Can you package your product as a gift?
- Collect your clients' information and maintain a database. And send them offers from time to time.
- Look a bit beyond your target audience. Target the audience that gives gifts to your main target audience, and ask them to come to your store before holidays.
- Give gift certificates before the holiday season. This will make your target audience come and do their holiday shopping at your store.

■ Repeat your offers. Max received a higher response because he followed up his letter offer with a postcard!

Lead Letters

Cris Parsons is a talented graphic designer. He has his own studio in Sunnyvale, California. To get new clients, he simply used to mail lead generation letters to executives in tech companies. The only purpose of these letters is to seek appointments.

If the executive didn't call Cris up and set an appointment after reading the lead generation letter, Cris would then follow up and call them himself a few days after sending his letter. This worked fairly well for Cris in getting steady work. Anytime work was slow, he would simply mail a bunch of letters to companies in Sunnyvale and then follow up by phone until he got a new client. One day, Cris got an idea. He made a change to his usual lead generation letters. He went and collected small stones' and stuffed them in the envelope. He then started his letter with the following headline: "Profit-building art direction and design are just a stone's throw away."

Because of adding the stone, his letters instantly became bulky and stood out from the bunch of other mail. More executives stopped just throwing it away with the rest of their junk mail. And way more of them actually picked up the phone and called Cris to schedule an appointment! This letter got Cris a few dozen appointments (instead of just a few) and kept him busy for a long time!

Action Summary:

■ Always follow up. If you have the resources and your prospect list is short, follow up by phone. If your prospect list is long, follow up by mail and then follow up again.

■ Use an attention-getting bulky yet cheap item in your mailings. A three-dimensional mailing will almost always get opened and read.

■ All you need is a bulky item and a connector that gives a reason to people why you are using that item in your mailings – and your response rate will more than double.

Two-Step Fax Marketing

Jeff Rubin helps other businesses in writing, editing and designing newsletters, brochures and other business communications. He used to use direct mail to generate new business. He would send mail to people, which would describe what he could do for them along with a bunch of testimonials from old clients. The business owners who received the direct mail piece could call Jeff and hire his services. This tactic generated business steadily. Jeff would receive a good average 1-1.5% response rate. (1% response rate is deemed as very good for most direct mail pieces!)

Then one day, Jeff sat down and wrote a report "How Too Produce Newsletters That Get Results." Jeff then sent a direct mail piece that contained just 2 pages. The first page described what the report reveals. And the 2nd page was a faxback form. If people would like to read Jeff's report for free, all they had to do was fill out the fax form with their details on it and fax it to Jeff.

Jeff would immediately mail his report to them, along with his sales letter that described his services. With this new 2-step process, Jeff's business exploded, as many as 20-30% of the people would fax back the form for the free report. And 20-30% of them would go on to hire Jeff. In all, Jeff enjoyed a cool 5-7% response rate because of his two-step process!

Action Summary:

- Two-step marketing processes are always more expensive. But they work extremely well too. Most of the time, they work way better than one-step direct selling processes. Especially if you are selling a product about which you have to educate the prospect a bit first.
- Write a report that educates the prospect while showing them that you are an expert. And then offer to send this report to people for free.
- Along with this report, also send a sales letter that sells your services.
- And then follow up with prospects. Call them up to ask them if they understood the report and if they have any questions. Answer their questions. Show them you know your material. And then make the sale.

Solo Mailing

Ron Shandler is the head of baseballhq.com. The site started off with a baseball newsletter. But over the years, it has grown and now sells all sorts of products from forecasting tools to strategy essays and more. Early on, Shandler started promoting his online products through offline means. Besides running advertisements in magazines, he also used direct postal mail to promote the products.

In the beginning, he used direct mail to promote several of baseballhq.com's products together. His direct mail pieces were more like catalogs. And each product had its own unique URL where people could go and actually buy it. These mailings generated a decent 1.4% response rate. Out of every 100 people who received these mailings, 1.4 of them ended up buying something.

Then one day, Shandler tested out something different. Instead of promoting several of his products together, he selected just one product and decided to promote it solo. But because he was just promoting one product, he thought of keeping the costs of mailing low. And thus, instead of normal mail, he elected to do a postcard mailing. And this postcard featuring just one product resulted in a response rate of more than 4%!

Over the months, Shandler has retested postcard mailings for different products and gets a good 4.1% response rate on average! He has not only reduced his mailing costs by using postcards, but his profits have grown by just promoting one product at a time too!

Action Summary:

- Most business owners think that as long as they are paying for an ad, they might as well promote all their products together. This rarely works well.

- Time and again, it has been proven by many direct mail ad tests that promoting only one product at a time beats promoting several products together. In the next ad you run, try promoting just one product instead of your entire line of products.

- What if you still don't feel like promoting one product alone? Two things you can do:

  1. Promote your company instead of your products. For example: instead of promoting rings and necklaces and other jewelry, promote the good service and the 27 years of experience of the company.

  2. Categorize your products and then promote the category. For example: instead of promoting toothpaste and toothbrushes, promote dental hygiene products.

Selling Ancient Descramblers

Mike Vilkie is a VP of marketing at RS&I – a satellite TV equipment company. His company bought 3 truckloads of TV descramblers some time back. But because these descramblers are hard to integrate with the current RS&I technology, they are outdated and put out of use even before they are taken out of the truck. RS&I finds itself tied up with 3 truckloads full of descramblers – each one costing $500. Total investment tied up? A cool 1.5 million dollars!

Mike is asked to deal with the situation. After talking to a few engineers, Mike finds that cable operators might still want to buy these descramblers. Mike does what he is trained to do: he buys a huge mailing list of all the cable operators in the nation. He then designs a flashy-looking 3-fold brochure. The brochure offers a discount on the descramblers. He puts their 1-800 number on the brochure. And after approval from his CEO, he mails these brochures to all the cable operators in the country. What was the total cost of the entire brochure mailing campaign? $25,000. Total phone calls the brochure results in? A big fat 0!

About that time, Mike meets a marketing consultant and tells him the story. The consultant asks Mike: why don't you simply tell the truth? And that's what Mike decides to do. He sits down and writes a brutally-honest letter. He writes that RS&I is stuck with these descramblers. Their busiest time of the year is approaching, and they don't have warehouse space to store these descramblers. Because of that, the cable operators are given a special discount equivalent to what RS&I would have to pay to rent a new warehouse.

When Mike shows this letter to his CEO, he is laughed at. The CEO says that this letter would never work. But after a long debate, he agrees that they have to try something at least.

This time though, Mike doesn't mail the letter to the entire cable operators list. He just mails to 1000 of them. Two days after the letters are mailed, RS&I starts receiving the phone calls. Forty seven people call within a day and buy 200 descramblers! About 109 cable operators out of the 1000 end up calling within the week – a cool 11% response rate. And 32% of them end up buying on the phone. Most of them buy more than one descrambler. Almost 500 units are sold because of this first mailing to 1000 people.

Mike now mails the same letter to the entire list. And within a month of mailing, all 3 truckloads full of descramblers are sold off. In fact, because of the high demand generated by that letter, phone calls keep coming in and RS&I buys one more truckload of descramblers and this time, sells them at profit!

Action Summary:

- Two main things to learn from Mike and RS&I's mistakes. One – don't try to cover the truth with flash and hype. Be truthful and reveal your mistakes. This builds trust and ends up getting you more sales.
- Second – test everything. RS&I would have averted the situation in the first place if they would have ordered 5-6 descramblers to test instead of 3 truckloads of them. They could have also saved $25,000 by mailing their brochures to just a handful of the people on the list.
- The easiest way to save money is to test out ideas on a smaller scale first.

Sneaky Direct Mail Campaign

Pablo Naranjo is an eye doctor in San Juan, Puerto Rico. He spends a lot of money to buy a lasik operation machine for his clinic. To promote his lasik services, he goes to an advertising consultant. The consultant advises Pablo to run a newspaper ad campaign and then follow it up with a direct mail campaign. But Pablo doesn't want to spend so much money on advertisements. So he does something very sneaky.

He scraps the newspaper ad campaign completely. He keeps the direct mail campaign but makes a twist to it. Pablo writes a big headline on the envelopes, and makes sure that his phone number and return address are there on all the envelopes. The headline:

"Inside: How Painless Lasik Eye Technology Can Remove Your Glasses in 20 Minutes"

But then instead of writing a sales letter and mailing it in the envelopes, he sends the envelopes empty! Quite a few people call him up to let him know that the envelope was empty. This leads to a conversation about the headline itself and Pablo then goes on and sells them the lasik treatment.

Action Summary:

- This is a very sneaky idea. You could test it out if you wanted to save some money on your direct mail campaigns.
- Add a headline and your phone number on the envelope – and mail the envelope empty. People will be curious to know why the envelope was empty and what would ordinarily be in it. And if your headline is strong enough, they'll call you to find out more.
- This sneaky trick works because you are able to persuade better

through phone - where you can ask people questions and answer their objections - than through mail. But it's much better than cold calling, as whoever calls has qualified themselves by reading the headline and being curious about the offer.

Classified Ad Secrets

Melvin Powers is a mail order marketing legend. He has sold a few million copies of different books through classified ads and mail order ads. Over the years, Powers found that two-step curiosity classified ads work really well in generating leads and converting leads into sales.

He would run small classified ads that wouldn't tell anything about the product. Their ambiguity would make people extremely curious and they would respond to the ad. Then Powers would send them some of his sales material to generate sales. One ad Melvin Powers ran to sell his own book:

FAMOUS MAIL ORDER MILLIONAIRE
reveals his money-making secrets.
Free, exciting details.
Write: <address>

This ad worked well. But then Powers made one small change to the ad which improved his response rates even further. His new ad read:

FAMOUS MAIL ORDER MILLIONAIRE
reveals his money-making secrets.
Free, exciting one-hour cassette.
Write: <address>

This small change more than doubled the orders his two-step classified ads generated!

Action Summary:

- Be specific in your ads. The more specific you are, the more believable your ads become and the higher the responses you'll get.
- Classified ads still work today. Try running two-step classified ads in relevant newspapers to see if there is a demand for your product in new markets.

Attention to Direct Marketing Detail

Nick Usborne is a very successful copywriter. Early on in his career, he was asked to beat a control of a brochure. ("Control" simply means current standard or current winner in direct marketing lingo.) The brochure promoted and sold a book on the topic of US forces in Vietnam.

Nick's client expected that he would overhaul the brochure totally and write more powerful headlines and gripping copy. But Nick read the brochure and found one unnecessary thing in it. He saw that the captions under pictures in that brochure were redundant. They didn't tell anything that the picture didn't already convey.

So Nick sat down and simply changed the captions. For example: there was one picture that showed an American Tunnel Rat entering a Vietcong tunnel system. The old caption for that photo was: "At the entrance of the tunnel system." Nick changed it to: "Tunnel rat tenses before plunging into darkness." (Nick used powerful verbs like "tenses" that describe feelings to make the captions more powerful and touching.) Nick didn't make any other major changes and somehow convinced his client to mail the new brochures. And these new brochures did beat the old controls!

Action Summary:

- Even before headlines, people's eyes revert to the photo in a sales letter. And the next thing their eye focuses on is the caption of the image. So make sure you use captions for every photo in your marketing pieces. And make sure that these captions are exciting.
- Use verbs in your captions to describe the photos. Verbs engage emotions of readers.
- A restaurant owner added captions under the photos of food dishes in his menu describing how the people would feel eating the food. And he found that more people ordered the dishes shown in the menu – even though these dishes were generally the most expensive dishes in the restaurant.

Pub Marketing

Café Flater is a small pub in a medium-sized city in the Netherlands. It was an average pub doing OK business, until Bob Ginkel became its manager.

Bob observed that more than half the pub visitors were students. Students would come in and spend a lot of time, but very little money at the pub. So Bob did a couple of things. First, he increased the entry fee to enter the pub. This got rid of many of the students who didn't have a lot of money to spend. Second, he contacted a few clothing stores and entered into a joint venture with them.

Bob specifically targeted the higher-end clothing stores, which either sold designer clothes or branded and expensive clothes. And he asked these store owners and managers to sell their list of clients to him.

Bob then sent a letter to all the clients and told them why they should come and visit Café Flater. Bob also included 2 coupons with the letter. Anyone could come to the pub and get free entry if they showed the coupon at the entrance. Bob specifically didn't rent mailing lists from the many mom-and-pop clothes shops. He only wanted to target people who had 2 qualities:

1. *They wore nice, fashionable clothes*
2. *They had money to spend*

And slowly but surely these people came and redeemed the coupons. Soon, Café Flater was filled with rich people wearing chic clothes instead of students wearing jeans and t-shirts. Within 6 months, Café Flater had become the place to go to in the entire town!

Action Summary:

- Decide on a target audience. Select a target audience of people who are "willing" and "able" to buy your products and services.
- Then determine where your target audience hangs out. Go approach these businesses and ask them if they could allow you to contact these people.
- Make use of "entry fees" and other such barriers to qualify people. Only do business with the target audience you've selected.
- Also, make use of coupons and freebie offers to attract people to come to you. People are generally lazy and won't change their habits easily. So give them a free sample or a trial offer they can't refuse.

Postcard Referral Strategy

Green Gear Cycling Company has an interesting idea that it uses to generate more referrals for its high-priced bikes. They used to rely on press releases and ads to generate sales. But now they solely focus on generating business through word-of-mouth sales.

Over the past few years, they have opened 30 "Bike Friday clubs" in America, Europe and Australia. (The club is named after Green Gear's signature cycle called "Bike Friday.") To start the clubs, Green Gear mailed a letter to everyone in a 60-mile radius of a city asking if they wanted to join the club for free. Many did join to interact with like-minded bikers.

Green Gear then also sent 12 prepaid postcards to each of the members of its clubs. When someone asks a biker about their bikes, they could give them a postcard. The interested person could then fill their names and addresses on the postcard and drop it in their mailbox. Green Gear would then send a brochure with more information to the interested person. And if a sale were made, Green Gear would also give $50-75 credit to the person who referred their friends. These referral credits can then be used to buy Green Gear accessories or even a second bike.

The postcard referral strategy has worked extremely well for Green Gear – bringing in close to 3500 new clients. Over the last 3 years, it has helped generate sales of 1.3 million dollars! Their best client referred 100 people who bought bikes worth $300,000!

Action Summary:

- You could copy the same referral strategy too. Give away prepaid postcards to your clients. Your clients can give these postcards to their friends who could fill them up with their contact details and post them to receive more information about your company.

- You could also give your clients referral credit as an incentive to be proactive in referring others to you.

- If you don't already have a database, start building one. If you do have a database of clients, mail them and start a community for them. They can meet up three to four times a year and interact and bond.

- Bonding with each other will make them bond with your company too.

Offline Wish Lists

Dusty Simmons owns a retail store that sells surfing products and beach supplies in Florida. But he faced some stiff competition. Because all the other surfing stores carried the same inventory and were situated in close proximity to each other, Dusty had a hard time differentiating his store from others.

People would just end up buying from the first store they entered. Dusty wanted to out-sell his competition - especially during the Christmas vacations. Dusty custom printed blank wish lists. These wish lists provided blank lines that people could fill in with the names of the products they wanted to buy. Each of these wish lists mentioned Dusty's store address too.

Dusty then asked kids who came to his store to window shop to fill out these wish lists. He then asked them to write their parents' names and addresses on an envelope. Dusty would then insert the wish lists with another special letter into the envelopes and mail them.

The special letter sent out with every wish list asked parents to show up to Dusty's store for a 3-hour special event with free drinks, snacks and music after the normal store hours on a specified day. Those three hours became the best three hours for Dusty's store. He sold more products in those 3 hours than he would sell in 1 whole week!

The 3-hour special was such a big hit that people who didn't make it started asking Dusty if he planned any more such events in the future. So Dusty started hosting these 3-special events every year before Christmas. And his sales have always been stellar during these 3 hours!

Action Summary:

- Use the power of wish lists for your own shop too. Print out a few blank wish lists and give it to everyone while they are leaving your store.
- Wish lists are a great pre-emption idea. You will make people to come to your stores to do their gift shopping rather than going to your direct competition, or even shops that sell products not related to your industry.
- Wish lists have one more advantage: it allows you to create a database of people.
- You could also of course send these blank wish lists with a stamp attached to it to your current clients by mail.

Power Picture

Julie is a fashion designer. She started selling her designer clothes to local shops. Bit by bit, she saved enough money to open her own small boutique.

Her business was doing well, but there was a lot of room for improvement. So Julie hired a marketing consultant who could help her revamp her brand and increase sales. Among several suggestions, one good suggestion the consultant gave Julie was to start collecting mailing information from her clients and then send them a brochure showing her new designs 4 times a year.

Julie started sending a quarterly brochure with 12-14 sketched designs regularly, and saw many of her clients coming back to her regularly. Some of her clients simply started calling Julie and ordering the clothes over the phone for home delivery.

The return on investment was well worth the time and money spent on producing the simple brochures. But then, one day, Julie did something that increased her brochure response by a cool 30%!

What did she do? Instead of using design sketches in her brochures, Julie hired models to pose in her designed clothes in natural surroundings ... in rooms and gardens and restaurants. And that change alone boosted her sales by 30%!

Action Summary:

- Models wearing clothes worked as a "testimonial" for Julie. Instead of just showing a picture of your product, show real people using your products and your sales should increase too.
- Ask your clients to provide you with their pictures using your product. And use those pictures along with their testimonials to sell your wares.

Last call for alcohol...

it's how I know we are coming to the end.

So with the turd having been dropped on the importance of planning out a strategy before you spend a dime marketing your company, take time to look at the three worlds of business that changes can be made in. Create a plan of action that will move your company forward and grow loyal customers. Choose a path, a position to hold and make all your marketing support this choice. Have your advertising, policies, social media, Internet and staff all aligned to sing the same song.

Some of the case studies created dramatic changes quickly, some took longer to cause change, but all of them moved the needle. Use the brainstorming techniques to look at the world inside your business, the world of your customer and the world of the competition and see where you can make the biggest leaps. There are certainly risks involved and not every strategy will work in each market. Some plans that worked might not be effective in your market. You must always bring in the wild card, the expertise and market knowledge of the company owner and marketing people.

Whether you are one of those marketing salespeople who wants to be better or one of those marketing creatives who wants to be more creative, take these brainstorming techniques, methods and case studies and make them part of your tool box to improve marketing and advertising.

If you're a business owner, then observe the areas in your company that can be modified to move it to the next level. Be willing to step outside of the box, instead of just talking about it. There was risk in starting a business; there is also risk in growing it. You won't get great success unless you go for it, but you already knew that.

For any of those bizarre people who just picked up a marketing book because it seemed like a good read, you're our kind of crazy. I encourage you (as well as the other three groups) to look at some of the Wizard of Ads books and take a trip to Wizard Academy in Austin, Texas for a day full of brain candy. It's a school of the communication arts (wizardacademy.com). Ankesh and I met during a class at Wizard Academy. We started a lifelong friendship based around a love of marketing. We hope you enjoy our first project and have found at least one strategy or case study that will take your business to the next level.

Good luck and good marketing!

You can follow up and learn more about the authors, or start a conversation at: www.mikekeesee.com and www.ankeshkothari.com. Follow along with us at our blog: www.TheStrategyDaddy.com (This is my invite to join us at our social media platform.)

About the Authors

Michael Keesee

Michael Keesee is a business strategist and Wizard of Ads partner guaranteed to make many business people uncomfortable. Mike, a veteran of television and radio, has a reputation for shaking up business models to create successful positioning and sales strategies that produce results for small business. Mike's creative genius and ability to see opportunity is endless and with a career in broadcast that has spanned from account executive to VP and General Manager, Mike has an infinite supply of marketing challenges to fine tune his craft and marketing experience. Raised in Lawton, Oklahoma and having spent most of his career in Texas, Mike values a beautiful day, a good glass of wine and a great problem solving conversation. Mike makes his home in the Grand Cayman Islands, and spends most of his time helping small companies do great things with their marketing and working with world class sales and marketing teams.

Ankesh Kothari

- Can't small talk
- Disorganized
- But gets the things done
- Voracious reader
- Born with a very curious mind
- Makes other people cook for him
- Part time writer
- Full time gopher
- Currently resides in Mumbai, India
- Sunsign: Aries
- Started his first venture at the age of 15
- Serial entrepreneur
- Loves travelling
- Has traveled extensively all over India, North America and Western Europe
- Loves collecting quotes
- Tends to write in bullet points sometimes
- Awesome at strategy and planning
- MBTI personality: INTx
- Loves chocolates!
- Good at finding solutions to hard problems